Dictionary of Chemistry

Dictionary of Chemistry

Taniya Sachdeva

Published by
PRABHAT PRAKASHAN PVT. LTD.
4/19 Asaf Ali Road,
New Delhi-110 002 (INDIA)
e-mail: prabhatbooks@gmail.com

ISBN 978-93-5048-498-2
DICTIONARY OF CHEMISTRY
by Taniya Sachdeva

Edition
2025

Price
₹ 500.00 (Rupees Five Hundred only)

Printed at
Narula Printers, Delhi

★ ❊ ★ ❊ ★

I would like to dedicate
this book to my Parents,
who are like God-figures to me
and nurtured me what I am.

★ ❊ ★ ❊ ★

Contents

Abegg's rule

Also known as Abegg's law of valence and countervalence, it is a rule stating that the addition of the maximum positive and negative valences of an element is frequently eight.

Abel tester

It is an instrument used in laboratories to test the flash points of volatile oils, like kerosene, which have flash points below120°F or 49°C.

Abherent

Also known as release agent, it is a chemical used to get a slip effect. It can be put to use in processes involving mold release, die-cast release, plastic release, etc.

Ab-initio calculation

It is the way through which atomic and molecular structure is computed as deduced from the solution of the Schrödinger equation of the molecule in question.

Absolute

This refers to something that is perfect or complete or pure; something that is not relative to anything else.

Absolute alcohol

Also referred to as ethyl alcohol, ethanol, anhydrous alcohol, it is alcohol with a low water content, ranging from 1% to ppm (parts per million) levels. It is used in medicines, perfumes, cleaning solutions and rocket fuel.

Absolute boiling point

It is the boiling point of a substance asdenoted in the unit of an absolute (thermodynamic) temperature scale.

Absolute configuration

Synonymously called absolute stereochemistry, it is the three-dimensional, spatial arrangement of the atoms of a chiral molecular entity and its stereochemical description.

Absolute entropy

It is the increase in entropy of a substance as it goes from absolute zero (0 K) to the temperature in question. With the use of the third law of thermodynamics, the values of absolute entropies of different substances can be assessed.

Absolute gravity

Also known as absolute density, it is a value that denotes the density or specific gravity at standard conditions. For instance, the standard atmospheric pressure at 0°C is the standard condition in the case of gases.

Absolute reaction rate

The reaction rate determined from statistical thermodynamics, using the assumption of the theory of absolute reaction rates.

Absolute temperature

It is another name for thermodynamic temperature, which is measured on an absolute scale (Celsius or Fahrenheit).

Absolute zero

Through the means of thermodynamics, it is the temperature at which molecular motion stops and reaches the zero point (0 K, or –273.15°C, or –459.67°F) on the absolute temperature scale.

Absorption

It is a process in which one substance aborbs in another, for instance, a gas dissolved by a liquid or solid, or a fluid absorbed in a liquid or solid.

Absorption coefficient

Also known as molar absorption coefficient (spectroscopy), it is a measure of the rate denoting the intensity of electromagnetic radiation as light, as it passes through a substance or material.

Absorption limit

Synonymous with absorption edge, it is a discontinuity in the graph of the absorption coefficient of a substance plotted against the wavelength of x-rays being absorbed.

Absorption spectrum

It is a spectrum related to the absorption of electromagnetic radiation by atoms or other entities resulting from shifts from lower to higher energy levels.

Absorption tower

A vertical equipment used to divide and classify components of a rising gas with the help of a falling liquid (often water) to trap and absorb the gas. Also known as scrubbers, this tower is put to use mainly in the industries in a variety of settings for purification, processing of materials, and other activities.

Abstraction

It is a chemical reaction where the bimolecular removal of a neutral or charged atom or ion from a molecule takes place.

Accelerator

Simply known as a catalyst, this substance speeds up the rate of chemical reaction.

Accelerator mass spectrometer

This is a research instrument used to accelerate streams of charged sub-nuclear particles to high velocities in order to classify and evaluate them, and is now used to count carbon isotope atoms for radiocarbon dating also.

Acceptor

This is an atom or molecule which acquires one or more electrons from another atom or molecule, leading to a coordinate chemical bond.

Accessory pigment

Any pigment in plants that can absorb light energy and pass the electrons along to the primary pigment (chlorophyll *a*), which leads to the chemical process of photosynthesis. Other forms of this pigment are chlorophyll *b, c, d,* and also non-chlorophyll accessory pigments such as carotenoids.

Accumulator

It is a kind of secondary cell or storage battery, which is recharged by passing electric current through it from an external direct current supply. During this process, the chemical reactions in the cell are reversed by the charging current. Some of the known ones are the lead-acid accumulator, the nickel-cadmium cell, etc.

Accumulator (secondary cell; storage battery)

A type of voltaic cell or battery that can be recharged by passing a current through it from an external d.c. supply. The charging current, which is passed in the opposite direction to that in which the cell supplies current, reverses the chemical reactions in the cell. The common types are the lead-acid accumulator and the nickel-iron and nickel-cadmium accumulators.

Accuracy

It shows how closely a measured value agrees with the correct value.

Acenaphthene [$C_{12}H_{10}$]

It is a colourless, unsaturated, polycyclic aromatic hydrocarbon (PAH), which consists of naphthalene with an ethylene bridge connecting positions 1 and 8. It is used in the production of dyes, pesticides and medicines.

Acene

It is a polycyclic aromatic hydrocarbon, made of fused benzene rings in rectilinear order.

Acenocoumarol [$C_{19}H_{15}NO_6$]

Also referred to as acenocoumarin, it is a coumarin that is used as an anticoagulant, functioning like warfarin (a vitamin K antagonist). It is a slightly soluble, crystalline powder, having no odour or taste, and has a melting point of 197°C.

Acephate [$C_4H_{10}NO_3PS$]

Acephate is an organophosphate foliar insecticide, used mainly for controlling a wide range of plant pests, including aphids, budworms, and tent caterpillars. It is utilised in the form of pressurized aerosol, emulsifiable concentrates, tree injection systems, etc.

Acetal [$CH_3CH(OC_2H_5)_2$]

This is an organic compound formed by adding alcohol molecules to aldehyde molecules. It is an inflammable, colourless liquid, which is commonly used in the preparation of cosmetics, and also as a solvent for dissolving other substances.

Organic compounds formed by addition of alcohol molecules to aldehyde molecules.

Acetaldehyde [CH_3CHO]

Also known as ethanal, it is a colourless, volatile liquid and is used for the production of solvents, reducing agents, acetic acid, sleep-inducing drugs, etc.

Acetal resin

It has many names: polyoxymethylene, polyacetal, and polyformaldehyde. This is produced by the addition polymerisation of aldehydes through the carbonyl function, creating polyoxymethylene chains. These synthetic resins are mainly utilized as an engineering thermoplastic, used in precision parts.

Acetamide [CH_3CONH_2]

Synonymous with ethanamide, it is the simplest crystalline amide of acetic acid produced by dehydrating ammonium acetate. This organic compound is used as industrial solvents and plasticizers.

Acetanilide [$C_6H_5NH\ (COCH_3)$]

This is an odourless, crystalline chemical, generated through a reaction of acetic anhydride with aniline. It is used for various purposes, for example, in the production of dyes and rubber, as a painkiller in medicines, etc.

Acetate

Also known as ethanoate, it is derived from acetic acid. Acetate includes salts and esters, as well as the anion found in solution.

Acetic acid [CH_3COOH]

This organic compound is also known as ethanoic acid. It is a colourless liquid with a sour taste and a distinctive odour. Vinegar is a diluted form of acetic acid; which when undiluted, is called glacial acetic acid.

Acetic anhydride [$(CH_3CO)_2O$]

This anhydride of acetic acid is a colourless liquid with an acrid smell. Also known as ethanoic anhydride, it is primarily used for acetylations, which is further used in photographic films, coated materials, etc.

Acetine [C_3H_5 $(OH)_2OOCCH$]

Commonly known as acetin, it is a product of acetic acid and glycerin when heated together. It is a syrupy, colourless, hygroscopic liquid, which is used in dyes, explosives, etc.

Acetoacetic acid [CH_3COCH_2COOH]

This unstable organic compound is also called 3-oxobutanoic acid, which can be prepared by the hydrolysis of the ethyl acetoacetate followed by acidification of the anion.

Acetoacetic ester

Other names of this organic compound are ethyl 3-oxobutanoate and ethyl acetoacetate. This colourless liquid with a pleasant smell boils at 181°C, and is used as a chemical intermediate, agent, and solvent.

Acetone [$(CH_3)_2CO$]

This organic compound, also known as propanone, is a colourless, mobile, flammable liquid, which is mixable in water. It is used as asolvent. It has medical and domestic uses.

Acetone cyanohydrin [$(CH_3)_2C(OH)CN$]

This is the cyanohydrin of acetone made from acetone and hydrogen cyanide. This extremely volatile, colourless liquid is used for the preparation of other cyanohydrins, as an intermediate, and in insecticides.

Acetone pyrolysis

It is the thermal decomposition of acetone into ketene.

Acetonitrile [CH_3CN]

This chemical compound, also called ethanenitrile, is a colourless liquid, which is primarily used in purification of butadiene, and as a solvent in organic synthesis.

Acetophenone [$C_6H_5C(O)CH_3$]

This organic compound, also known as phenyl methyl ketone, is colourless, viscous liquid, which is used in perfumes, pharmaceuticals.

Aceturic acid [$CH_3CONHCHCH_2COOH$]

It is a crystalline acid, which produces stable salts with organic bases. It is dissolvable in water and alcohol and is used in the pharmaceutical industry.

Acetyl

It is the organic group of acetic acid (CH_3CO–). Also called acetyl group, comprises a methyl group single-bonded to a carbonyl.

Acetylating agent

It is a chemical agent, synonymous with ethanoylating agent, which is able to bind an acetyl group onto an organic molecule.

Acetylation

Also known as actylation, it is a reaction that introduces an acetyl functional group into a chemical compound.

Acetyl chloride [CH_3COCl]

An acid chloride, also called ethanoyl chloride, is produced by the reaction of acetic acid with standard inorganic chlorodehydrating agents. This colourless liquid with a pungent smell is used mainly in preparing acetyl derivatives.

Acetylene [C_2H_2]

This chemical compound, also known as ethyne, is a colourless, explosive gas. This hydrocarbon is used in the manufacture of organic chemicals, as a fuel, forcutting and welding metals, etc.

Acetylide

It is any compound formed from acetylene by the replacement of one or both of its hydrogen atoms by a metal.

Acetyl propionyl [$CH_3COCOCH_2CH_3$]

It is a yellow-coloured liquid, with a boiling point of 106-110°C.

Acheson process

In this industrial process, the mixture of coke and clay is heated to make graphite.

Achiral molecules

A molecule which is not chiral. It happens when an improper rotation, that is a combination of a rotation and a reflection in a plane, perpendicular to the axis of rotation, results in the same molecule.

Acid

It is a sour-tasting substance which reacts with a base, and neutralises alkalis, dissolves some metals, and turns blue litmus red. Aqueous acids have a pH of less than 7, where an acid of lower pH is generally stronger. Some commonly known acids are acetic acid, hydrochloric acid, etc.

Acid anhydride

Also known as acyl anhydride, it is formed when the oxide of a nonmetal or compound reacts with water, and there is a removal of one or more water molecules in the process. It is used as an industrial chemical and is also a precursor to resins.

Acid-base indicator

This is a large organic molecule, which does respond to a change in the hydrogen ion concentration. Most of these are themselves weak acids or bases used to determine acidity or basicity of a solution.

Acid dye

It is a dye soluble in water, and is chemically a sodium salt of a sulphuric, carboxylic or phenol organic acid. It has found its uses in the textile industry (silk, nylon, etc.), and is also used as a food colourant.

Acid halide

This chemical compound, also called acyl halide, is obtained from an oxoacid by replacing a hydroxyl group with a halide group.

Acidic

It is (i) being or containing an acid; (ii) yielding an acid in aqueous solution.

Acidimetry

It is a volumetric analysis, where the amount of acid in a solution is determined, using an acidimeter or by titration.

Acid rain

It is any form of precipitation like rain, fog, snow, or hail that has noxious substances (nitrogen and sulphur oxides).

Acid reaction

An acid produces this chemical reaction.

Acid salt

It is a chemical compound constituted by the partial neutralisation of a dibasic or tribasic acid. This salt containing an ionizable hydrogen atom is used in food preparation, especially in baking.

Acid value

Also known as acid number or neutralization number, it is to quantify the amount of carboxylic acid groups in a chemical compound.

Acridine [$C_{12}H_9N$]

It is a colourless solid derived from the anthracine fraction of coal tar. This organic compound is used mainly in the synthesis of dyes and drugs.

Acrolein [CH_2=CHCHO]

Systematically named propenal, it is a clear liquid with an annoying, pungent smell. This unsaturated aldehyde is produced industrially from propylene, and used as a biocide, in medicines, etc.

Acrylamide [CH_2=$CHCONH_2$]

It is a white, odourless, crystalline solid, also known as acrylic amide, which is prepared on an industrial scale by the hydrolysis of acryl onitrile by nitrile hydratase. This chemical compound is chiefly used in synthesizing polyacrylamides, and also in making paper, wastewater treatment, etc.

Acrylate

Synonymous with propenoate, it is (i) derived from acrylic acid; (ii) an ester or salt of propenoic acid.

Acrylic acid [$CH_2CHCOOH$]

Another name for propenoic acid, this organic compound is colourless and has a pungent smell. This unsaturated carboxylic acid is used in the production of various plastics, coatings, adhesives, etc.

Acrylic resins

It is a group of related thermoplastics (resins) generated through chemical reaction by applying polymerization initiator and heat to a monomer. They are used mainly in inks, adhesives, synthetic plastics, pharmaceuticals, etc.

Acrylonitrile [CH_2CHCN]

This colourless liquid has an acrid smell, and it is used in the production of artificial fibers, rubbers and other polymers.

Actinium [Ac]

The atomic number of this soft, silvery-white radioactive chemical element is 89. It is rarely found as in uranium ores as an impurity. It has found its uses in medicine, and is a source of alpha rays.

Actinoids

Another name for acitinides, it is a series covering 15 metallic chemical elements with atomic numbers from 89 to 103.

Actinometry

It is a process of assessing and measuring the intensity of electromagnetic (incident) radiation with the help of actinometer (measuring instrument).

Activated complex

Another name for activated-complex theory, this theory points to a group of intermediate structures in a reaction that remain, while bonds are breaking and new bonds are taking form.

Activation energy

It is the amount of energy that must be taken in by reactants in their ground states to reach the transition state, so that a reaction can take place.

Active centre

Also known as active site, it is the portion of an enzyme where the catalytic activity on the substrate occurs.

Active metal

It is a metal with low ionization energy that loses electrons readily to form positively charged ions.

Activity

It is a thermodynamic amount that in a non-ideal solution denotes the effective concentration of a solute (dissolved matter).

Activity series

Also called electromotive series, it is a listing of metals according to their decreasing reactivity.

Actual yield

It is the quantity of a specified pure product actually acquired from a given reaction.

Acylation

It is a chemical process, where there is an incorporation of an acyl group into a compound (molecule).

Adamantane [$C_{10}H_{16}$]

This polycyclic hydrocarbon is a colourless, crystalline solid with a peculiar camphor-like odour and structure resembling a diamond lattice. This chemical compound is used in polymeric materials, drugs, etc.

Addition polymerisation

Also called polyaddition, it is a technique where many monomers (molecules) come together to form the growing polymer (long-chain polymers).

Addition reaction

It is an organic reaction, where two or more molecules bond together for the formation of a larger one.

Adduct

The formation of this chemical compound takes place through addition reaction.

Adhesive

It is a material which binds surfaces together. Generally, it is liquid or semi-liquid substance, which is derived from natural or man-made sources.

Adiabatic approximation

It denotes that the solution of Schrödinger equation at one time goes uninterruptedly over to the solution at a later time. An example of adiabatic approximation, used in quantum mechanics, is Born–Oppenheimer approximation.

Adipic acid [$(CH_2)_4(COOH)_2$]

This white crystalline powder is a dicarboxylic acid, which is hardly found in nature. This organic compound is used mainly in the manufacture of nylon and polymers.

Adrenaline

This neurotransmitter and hormone, called epinephrine, is an internal secretion by the adrenal glands in the body. It has found its application as a drug to help in the cases of heart attack, superficial bleeding, etc.

Adsorbent

It is a material, mostly poriferous, with a surface area that can adsorb substances. Some adsorbents are activated charcoal, water, metals, etc.

Adsorption

Synonymous with surface assimilation, this takes place when there is an accumulation of gases, liquids on the surface of a solid or liquid.

Adsorption indicator

It is an indicator used in a solution to detect excess of a substance or ion: in a precipitation reaction it points to an excess of a reactant.

Adsorption isotherm

It is an illustration of the connection between the bulk activity of adsorbate and the amount adsorbed at constant temperature.

Adulterant

It is a material that makes another substance impure by diluting it with extraneous, improper ingredients.

Aerosol

It is a cloud of solid or liquid particles suspended in gas.

AES (Auger electron spectroscopy)

A technique of chemical analysis, atomic emission spectroscopy, that uses the intensity of light emitted from a flame, plasma, spark, etc. at a specific wavelength to ascertain the quantity of an element.

Affinity chromatography

This is a technique of splitting up biochemical mixtures and is based on a highly specific interaction like the one between receptor and ligand.

Air

A mixture of many gases, mainly of oxygen and nitrogen, this invisible gas envelopes the earth.

Alcohol

It is a hydrocarbon derivative containing an –OH group attached to a carbon atom, not in an aromatic ring.

Hydrocarbon derivative containing an –OH group attached to a carbon atom not in an aromatic ring.

Aldehyde

It is a compound in which an alkyl or arly group and a hydrogen atom are attached to a carbonyl group. Its general formula is O-R-C-H.

Aldohexose

It is a monosaccharide sugar comprising six carbon atoms and an aldehyde group such as glucose or mannose.

Aldol reaction

Also known as aldol condensation, it is a way of forming carbon–carbon bonds in organic chemistry. It combines two carbonyl compounds to make a new β-hydroxy carbonyl compound, which is called aldol.

Algin

It is a viscid polysaccharide drawn out from certain brown algae. Its derivatives such as sodium alginate or alginic acid, are used as emulsifiers, suspending agents, etc.

Aliphatic compounds

It is a category of organic compounds whose carbon atoms are linked with each other in straight or branched open chains rather than in rings. Such compounds are the hydrocarbons of the alkane, alkene, and alkyne series.

Alizarin [$C_{14}H_8O_4$]

It is an orange-red crystalline compound which occurs naturally in madder root, and is used in making red pigments and dyes.

Alkali

Another name for base, it is a class of water soluble mineral compounds with a pH greater than 7. It is used in the production of cosmetics and toiletries.

Alkali metals

These are the highly reactive, electropositive metals of Group IA (1), which have strong basic elements such as sodium (Na), potassium (K), rubidium (Rb), etc.

Alkalimetry

It is process of determining the strength of an alkali, where standard solutions of alkali are used to measure the amount of acid present.

Alkaline

It relates to or contains an alkali (pH>7).

Alkaline-earth metals

They are a group of metals (elements) comprising Group IIA of the periodic table: magnesium (Mg), calcium (Ca), barium (Ba), etc.

Alkaloids

They are a group of natural bases having nitrogen discovered in plants.

Alkanes [C_nH_{2n+2}]

Also known as paraffins, they are saturated hydrocarbons including methane, ethane, etc. They are chemical compounds consisting of hydrogen or carbon atoms bonded with only single bonds.

Alkenes

Also called olefins, they are unsaturated hydrocarbons (or organic molecules) that contain one or more carbon-carbon triple bonds.

Alkoxide

This compound, also known as alcoholate, is derived from an alcohol by replacing the hydrogen of the hydroxyl group with a metal.

Alkyd resin

This durable synthetic resin, produced by the condensation of polyhydric alcohols with polybasic acids, is mainly used in paints and other surface coatings.

Alkyl group

It is a group of atoms obtained from an alkane by the removal of one hydrogen atom.

Alkylation

This chemical process involves the transferring of an alkyl group from one molecule to another.

Alkylbenzene

It is a compound containing an alkyl group bonded to a benzene ring.

Alkynes

Another name for acetylene, these are unsaturated hydrocarbons having triple carbon-carbon bonds.

Allene [C_3H_4]

Also known as propadiene, it is an unsaturated, open-chained hydrocarbon with two double bonds.

Allotropes

Different forms of the same element in the same physical state.

Allotropy

Synonymous with allotropism, it is a physical property of some chemical elements which exist in multiple forms.

Alloy

This metal is made by a combination of two or more metallic (or non-metallic) elements, for instance, steel is an alloy of iron and carbon.

Allyl alcohol [CH_2=$CHCH_2OH$]

This unsaturated primary alcohol, also known as propenol, is water-soluble, colourless, toxic liquid.

Alpha particle

It is a positively charged particle in the helium nucleus, which is emitted by some radioactive materials.

Alpha position

It is the first position from a designated carbon atom in an organic molecule at which an atom or radical may be substituted.

Alum

A specific compound, and also a class of chemical compounds, it is a hydrated double sulphate of aluminum and potassium.

Alumina [Al_2O_3]

This oxide of aluminium is a white solid which occurs in crystalline form as the main component of corundum, etc.

Aluminate

It is a compound of alumina and a metallic oxide.

Aluminium [Al]

This silvery ductile metallic element is extracted from bauxite, and is the most abundant metal found in the earth's crust. Its atomic number is 13, and is widely used in the manufacturing of automobiles (trucks), packaging material (foil), etc.

Aluminium acetate [$Al(C_2H_3O_2)_3$]

This compound in the form of its normal salt is synonymous with aluminium ethanoate. It is a white, water-soluble, un-crystallized powder used primarily in the pharmaceutical industry (astringent, antiseptic, etc.).

Aluminium chloride [$AlCl_3$ or Al_2Cl_6]

This hydrophilic compound fumes in air and reacts in a volatile manner with water. It exists in the form of white to colourless hexangular crystals, and is used as an accelerator in chemical reactions.

Aluminium hydroxide [Al $(OH)_3$]

Derived from bauxite, it is a hydroxide salt form of aluminium. This white crystalline compound has various uses in the production of glass, anti-perspirant deodorants, etc.

Aluminium oxide [Al_2O_3]

It is the group of inorganic compounds with the chemical formula 23. An amphiprotic oxide, generally referred to as alumina, it is utilised in the manufacturing of ceramic products, paper, etc.

Aluminium potassium sulphate [$Al_2(SO_4)_3.K_2SO_4.24H_2O$]

Also known as potassium alum or potash alum, it is a water-soluble, colourless and odourless crystalline compound. Naturally occurring as kalinite (mineral), it is used in the manufacture of leather products.

Aluminium sulphate [$Al_2(SO_4)_3$]

It is a white crystalline, water-soluble salt (compound), which is used in the paper, textile industries, and is also used for treatment of sewage water.

Ambident

It describes a chemical species (a molecule or group) that has two alternative and distinguishable reactive centres, to either of which a bond may be made during a reaction. Describing a molecule or group that has two alternative and interacting reaction sites, to either of which a bond may be made during a reaction.

Americium [Am]

This chemical element is produced by the beta decay of an isotope of plutonium. It is a radioactive metal of the actinide series with atomic number as 95.

Amides

These are compound which contain the O-C-N group, and can be considered a derivative of ammonia in which one or more hydrogens are replaced by an alkyl group.

Amidol [$C_6H_3(NH_2)_2OH.2HCl$]

It is a colourless crystalline compound (dihydrogen chloride salt), which is used mainly as a chemical agent for developing photographs.

Amines

They are derivatives of ammonia, where one or more hydrogen atoms have been replaced by organic groups.

Amino acid

It is an organic compound that contains both amino and carboxylic acid group, and is used in the manufacture of plastics, drugs, etc.

Ammine

It is a complex inorganic compound having ammonia molecules.

Ammonia [NH_3]

This colourless gas with a peculiar acrid smell is compounded of nitrogen and hydrogen. It is soluble in water and alcohol, and is used as a chemical intermediate and in fertilizers.

Ammonium bicarbonate [NH_4HCO_3]

This inorganic compound, also known as ammonium hydrogencarbonate, it is a colourless solid. Produced by compounding carbon dioxide and ammonia, it is used chiefly in the food industry.

Ammonium chloride [NH_4Cl]

Also called sal ammoniac, it is a white crystalline, water-soluble compound, which is used as a mordant, expectorant and soldering flux.

Ammonium nitrate [NH_4NO_3]

It is a white crystalline chemical compound, which is used in fertilizers and some explosives.

Ammonium sulphate [$(NH_4)_2SO_4$]

Made by treating ammonia, this inorganic colourless salt is used for various commercial purposes such as soil fertilizers.

Ammonium thiocyanate [NH_4SCN]

A salt of the ammonium cation and the thiocyanate anion, this inorganic compound is used as a stabilizing agent in photography, and in the production of resins, matches, etc.

Amount of substance

Sometimes called chemical amount, it is a standard quantity that measures the size of a specified group of elementary entities such as atoms, molecules, electrons, etc.

Ampere

It is a unit of electrical current; 1 ampere equals 1 coulomb per second.

Amperometric titration

A kind of quantitative analysis, it describes a group of titrations in which the equivalence point is ascertained through measurement of the electric current generated by the titration reaction.

Amphiphile

Also referred to as amphiphilic or amphipathic, it is any compound having both hydrophilic and lipophilic properties.

Amphiprotic

Another name for amphoteric, it is a substance having features of both an acid and a base, and is capable of reacting as either.

Ampholyte

It is (i) an amphiprotic electrolyte; (ii) a molecule with a positive and a negative charge.

Amyl group

This is any of several univalent, isomeric groups with the formula C_5H_{11}–.

Anabolism

Synonymous with constructive metabolism, it is a metabolic synthesis of complex molecules in living organisms from simpler kinds together with the storage of energy.

Analysis

It is (i) the process of breaking down a substance into its constituent elements; (ii) an elaborate examination of the elements or structure of a substance. There are two types of analysis: quantitative and qualitative.

Anchimeric assistance

Also called neighbouring-group participation, it is the reciprocal action of a reaction centre with a lone pair of electrons in an atom or the electrons that exist in a sigma bond.

Angle-resolved photoelectron spectroscopy

Abbreviated as ARPES, it is a method of studying the electronic structure of the surface of solids. It is a form of spectroscopy in which photoelectrons are analyzed for their emission angle and kinetic energies.

Anharmonic oscillator

Used in classical or quantum mechanics, it is an oscillator that is not oscillating in simple harmonic motion.

Anhydride

It is the compound obtained by the removal of elements of water from an acid.

Anhydrous

A substance is anhydrous if it has little water or is waterless.

Aniline [$C_6H_5NH_2$]

Also known as phenylamine, it is the simplest aromatic amine. A colourless, oily, toxic liquid used for the production of dyes and medicines.

Animal charcoal

It is a black substance which contains char in the form of carbonized bone. Derived from the destructive distillation of organic material, it is used as a black pigment and also used to adsorb colouring physical entity.

Anion

It is (i) a negative ion; (ii) atom or group of atoms that has gained one or more electrons.

Anode

It is a positively charged electrode by which the electrons exit an electrical device.

Anomer

It is a cyclic stereoisomer, whose only configurational difference concerns the arrangement of atoms or groups in the aldehyde or ketone group.

Anti

In stereochemical relations, it stands contrary to being on the same side, and implies being on opposite sides of a reference plane.

Antiaromatic

Also known as pseudoaromatic, it is a cyclic compound containing an even number of alternating single and double bonds.

Antibiotics

It is any substance that can destroy or restrain the growth of bacteria and microorganisms.

Antifoaming agent

Synonymous with defoamer, it is a chemical additive that decreases and obstructs the formation of foam in industrial process liquids.

Antifreeze

The addition of this liquid to the water in a cooling system lowers its freezing point.

Antimony [Sb]

This chemical element, having four allotropic forms, is found in stibnite. It is a brittle silvery-white metalloid with its atomic number as 51, and is used in a wide variety of alloys.

Antioxidants

It is a substance that restrains oxidation (chemical reaction).

Aquation

It is a process in which a ligand is replaced by water in a complex.

Aqueous

It relates to, or is similar to, or contains water (generally as solvent or medium).

Argon [Ar]

It is an inert gas with its atomic number as 18, which lacks colour and odour, and comprises approximately 1% of the earth's atmosphere.

Aromatic compounds

This is a class of organic compounds, which contain one or more benzene rings.

Arsenate

It is (i) arsenic acid's salt or ester; (ii) a negative ion.

Arsenic [As]

This poisonous metallic element with 33 as its atomic number has three allotropic forms. This brittle steel-grey metalloid is used in manufacturing glass and as a pesticide.

Arsenic acid [H_3AsO_4]

Also known as orthoarsenic acid, it is a poisonous, white, translucent crystalline solid used in the production of arsenates.

Aryl group

It is a group of atoms remaining after a hydrogen atom is removed from the aromatic system.

Asbestos

It is a heat-resistant fibrous silicate mineral, which is used for fireproofing, electrical insulation, etc.

Aspirin

This synthetic compound is the acetylated derivative of salicylic acid, and is used as an analgesic drug.

Association

It is the process of combining of separate molecular entities into any aggregate.

Atom

It is the smallest particle of an element.

Atomic absorption spectroscopy

Abbreviated as AAS, it is an analytical method used to ascertain the concentration of a particular metal element in a sample.

Atomicity

It is the number of atoms in the molecules of an element.

Atomic mass unit

Also called unified mass unit or dalton, it is a unit used for denoting atomic and formula weights. It is one-twelfth of a mass of an atom of the carbon-12 isotope.

Atomic number

It is the integral number of protons in the nucleus, and also defines the identity of element.

Atomic weight

Also known as relative atomic mass, it is the weighted average of the masses of the constituent isotopes of an element.

Aufbau principle

This term literally means building up, and describes the order in which electrons fill orbitals in atoms.

Autocatalysis

It defines a state where the catalysis in which the catalyst is one of the products of the reaction.

Autoprotolysis

It is a proton transfer reaction between two similar molecules (one acting as a Brønsted acid and the other as a Brønsted base).

Avogadro's law Also known as Avogadro's hypothesis, it is a gas law according to which at the same temperature and pressure, equal volumes of all gases have the same number of molecules.

Azeotrope

Also known as azeotropic mixture, it is a solution (mixture) of two liquids that has a constant boiling point and composition during distillation. It retains the same composition and cannot be separated.

Azulene [$C_{16}H_{26}O$]

It is an oily, blue liquid, which is insoluble in water, and is used in cosmetics.

❑

Babo's law

Named after Lambert von Babo, it is a law which states that the vapour pressure of a solution is lowered in proportion to the amount of solute added.

Background radiation

It is a uniform microwave radiation remaining from the Big Bang and is extraneous to an experiment.

Back titration

This analytical chemistry method is a titration performed in reverse, where a known excess of standard chemical agent is added to the solution, and the excess is titrated.

Baking soda

Another name for sodium bicarbonate ($NaHCO_3$), it is a white crystalline solid, which has a slightly salty taste. This chemical compound is chiefly used in cooking, pharmaceutical industry, etc.

Balance

It is a device for weighing such as the simple beam balance (a central pivot, beam and a pair of scales).

Band

It is a series of closely spaced, almost continuous molecular orbitals that belong to the crystal as a whole.

Band of stability

It is a band which contains non-radioactive nuclides in a plot of number of neutrons versus atomic number.

Band theory of metals

This theory refers to the bonding and properties of metallic solids.

Barfoed's test

This chemical test is used for finding out the presence of monosaccharides.

Barium [Ba]

This soft, silvery-white, reactive metal of the alkaline earth group, with atomic number 56 is used in many alloys.

Barium carbonate [$BaCO_3$]

Also known as witherite, this white powder (chemical compound) is used in the manufacture of bricks, cement, etc.

Barium hydroxide [$Ba(OH)_2.8H_2O$]

This chemical compound of barium, also known as baryta, is the white granular monohydrate, which is used in making lubricating oils, soaps, etc.

Barometer

It is a device for measuring pressure.

Base

It is a substance that produces OH (aq) ions in aqueous solution. Strong bases are soluble in water and are totally dissociated; whereas weak bases ionise only in a slight manner.

Basic anhydride

It is the oxide of a metal that reacts with water to form a base.

Basic salt

It is a salt that contains an ionisable OH group.

Bathochromic shift

It is an alteration of spectral band position in the absorption, reflectance, and transmittance of a molecule to a longer wavelength.

Battery

It is an arrangement of two or more cells electrically connected together to generate electrical energy.

Beckmann rearrangement

Named after Ernst Otto Beckmann, it is an acid-catalyzed rearrangement of an oxime to an amide, which is used in the manufacturing nylon.

Beer-Lambert law

This law concerns with the absorption of light to the attributes of the material through which the light is passing.

Benedict's test

Also called Benedict's solution, this test is conducted to find out the presence of reducing sugars by heating the solution to be tested with Benedict's reagent.

Benzene [C_6H_6]

Also known as benzol, this organic chemical compound is a colourless and highly flammable liquid with a pleasant fragrance, and is used in chemical synthesis.

Benzoic acid [C_6H_5COOH]

Synonymous with benzenecarboxylic acid, it is a colourless crystalline solid found in benzoin and other plant resins. It is used in the food and pharmaceutical industry.

Benzoin [$C_6H_5CHOHCOC_6H_5$]

This balsamic resin is a colourless crystalline aromatic ketone used for making perfumes, medicines, etc.

Benzoylation

It is a reaction that involves the introduction of a benzoyl group into a molecule.

Benzylamine [$C_6H_5CH_2NH_2$]

Also known as aminotoluene and phenylmethylanine, it is a colourless, toxic, liquid base, and is used in organic synthesis.

Benzyne

A member of a group of compounds known as arynes, it is a highly reactive compound, which has a benzene ring with a triple bond.

Berkelium [Bk]

The atomic number of this radioactive metal is 97. This transuranic element of the actinide series was first created artificially by bombarding americium with helium ions.

Berthelot equation

It is a form of the equation of state that relates the temperature, pressure, and volume of a gas with the gas constant.

Berthollide compound

Belonging to the class of non-stoichiometric compounds, it is a solid chemical compound that cannot be restricted within the law of definite proportions.

Beryllium [Be]

This hard, grey-coloured metal does not oxidize at ordinary temperatures. This chemical element with atomic number 4 is used in radiation windows, mirrors, etc.

Beryllium oxide [BeO]

Also called beryllia, this formless, colourless, crystalline oxide is generally used as a refractory.

Beta particle

It is the electron emitted from the nucleus when a neutron decays to a proton and an electron.

Bicarbonate

It is a salt of carbonic acid (with the anion HCO_3^{-1}) in which one hydrogen atom has been substituted.

Bimolecular reaction

It is a chemical process in which two molecules react together resulting in the formation of a new-species.

Binary

It is anything which contains two components.

Binary acid

It is a binary compound in which H is bonded to one or more of the more electronegative non-metals.

Binary compound

It is a chemical compound consisting of exactly two different elements.

Biochemistry

It is (i) the branch of science related to compounds and processes occurring in organisms; (ii) an attempt to understand biology within the context of chemistry.

Biodegradability

It is the ability of a substance to be broken down into simpler substances by bacteria.

Bioreactor

It is an equipment (or apparatus) in which a biological reaction is performed mostly at industrial level.

Biosensor

It is an analytical device by which biological molecules (enzymes or antibodies) are used to detect the presence of chemicals.

Biotechnology

It is the study of molecular biology (microorganisms), where such knowledge can be used to perform specific industrial processes.

Biotin

It is a vitamin in the vitamin B group that is essential for body's growth.

Bismuth [Bi]

This colourless, crystalline, brittle, highly diamagnetic metallic element, with atomic number 83, is used in making alloys.

Bitumen

It is a thick, black mixture of hydrocarbons that occurs naturally or as a remainder from petroleum distillation.

Blast furnace

It is an enclosed chamber in the form of a tower into which a blast of hot compressed air is forced to enter from below. It is mainly used for smelting a mixture of iron ore, coke, and limestone to make iron.

Bleaching powder

It is a white powder comprised of calcium hydroxide, chloride and hypochlorite, used as a bleaching agent and disinfectant.

Boat confirmation

Being unstable in nature, it is a confirmation where carbons C2, C3, C5 and C6 are lying in the same direction, while C1 and C4 are moved (or replaced) away from that plane in the same direction.

Bohrium [Bh]

Created artificially by high-energy atomic collisions, it is an unstable, transuranic chemical element with atomic number 107.

Boiling point

Also called condensation point, it is the temperature at which the vapour pressure of a liquid is equal to applied pressure.

Boiling point elevation

It is the increase in the boiling point of a solvent due to the dissolution of a non-volatile solute.

Bond

Another name for chemical bond, it is any of the several forces by which atoms are bound in a molecule (ionic bond, metallic bond, etc.).

Bond dissociation energy

Simply stated it is the amount of energy needed to break a bond between two atoms. It is described as the standard enthalpy change when a bond is cleaved by homolysis.

Bond order

It is half the number of electrons in bonding orbitals subtracted by half the number of electrons in antibonding orbitals.

Bonding orbital

It is a molecular orbit lower in energy than any of the atomic orbitals of which it is a derivative.

Boric acid [H_3BO_3]

Synonymously called boracic acid and orthoboric acid, it is a white, mildly acid solid used for making heat-resistant glasses, adhesives, enamels, etc.

Boride

It is a compound in which the most electronegative element is boron (particularly a compound of boron and a metal).

Boron [B]

Extracted mainly from kernite and borax, this chemical element with atomic number 5, is a trivalent non-metallic solid. It is used in alloys, propellant mixtures, flares, etc.

Boron hydrides

Also known as borane, these are binary compounds of boron and hydrogen.

Born-Haber cycle

It is a chain of reactions which, when summed, denotes the hypothetical one-step reaction by which elements in their standard states are converted into crystals of ionic compounds.

Boyle's law

The law in which at constant temperature, the volume occupied by a definite mass of a gas is inversely proportional to the applied pressure.

Brass

It is a class of various metal alloys made chiefly of copper and zinc.

Breeder reactor

It is a nuclear reactor that generates more fissionable nuclear fuel than it consumes.

Bromate

It is a salt or ester of bromic acid, which has the univalent group $-BrO_3$ or ion BrO_3^-.

Bromide

It is a compound of bromine with another element, and is used as a sedative.

Bromine [Br]

A part of the halogen group, this chemical element has atomic number 35. This non-metallic, dark red-brown liquid element with a disagreeable odour is found as salts in seawater, and is used in producing many other compounds.

Bromothymol blue

Also called bromothymol sulphone phthalein, it is an acid-base indicator, in which the change in the colour indicates the shift (from acidic to basic).

Bronsted acid

It is a proton donor.

Bronsted base

It is a proton acceptor.

Bronze

It is a yellowish-brown-coloured alloy of copper with one-third tin (approx.) and is used for industrial and aesthetic purposes.

Brown-ring test

This is a test to detect the presence of nitrate ion, which is indicated by appearance of a brown ring at the end of the test.

Buckminsterfullerene [C_{60}]

It is a form of carbon containing molecules of 60 atoms organized in a polyhedron similar to a geodesic sphere.

Buffer

Also known as buffer solution, it comprises either a weak acid or a weak base, and which is unsusceptible to alterations in pH.

Bumping

It is a phenomenon in which a solvent becomes overheated, resulting in a sudden release of vapour bubble, driving liquid to flowout of the flask in an explosive manner.

Burette

It is a piece of volumetric glassware that is utilized to deliver solutions to be used in titrations in a quantitative way.

Butane [C_4H_{10}]

This member of the alkane series is a component of petroleum. It is an inflammable hydrocarbon gas, which is used as a fuel, and also in making rubber.

Butanol [C_4H_9OH]

Another name for butyl alcohol, it is an inflammable alcohol obtained from butane, and used as a solvent (resins), and for producing organic compounds.

Butene

Synonymous with butylenes, it is any of three isomeric hydrocarbons C_4H_8, used chiefly in the manufacture of synthetic rubbers.

Butler-Volmer equation

Applied in electrochemical kinetics, it explains how the electrical current on an electrode depends on the electrode's potential.

Butyl group

It is the hydrocarbon radical group with general chemical formula $-C_4H_9$.

Butyric acid [$CH_3CH_2CH_2$-COOH]

This organic acid, also called butanoic acid, is a thick, colourless liquid with a disagreeable odour and pungent taste. It is used in food as an additive, for preparing esters, etc.

❑

Cacodyl [$As_2(CH_3)_4$]

It is a poisonous oil, with a disagreeable garlic-like smell and belongs to the arsenic group $(CH_3)_2As$-.

Cadmium [Cd]

This metallic element, with atomic number 48, occurs in association with zinc ores. It is a bluish-white, malleable, poisonous, divalent element, which is used in cells, fittings, etc.

Cadmium sulphide [CdS]

Also called cadmium yellow and cadmium orange, it is naturally found as greenockite (mineral in crystalline form), and is used as a pigment.

Caffeine [$C_8H_{10}N_4O_2$]

It is an alkaloid compound found in many plants (coffee, tea, etc.), and soft drinks, and functions as a stimulant.

Cage effect

It is a process stating how the surroundings affect the properties of a molecule.

Calamine

It is a pink-coloured powder comprising zinc carbonate and ferric oxide, which is used for manufacturing lotions, ointments, etc.

Calcination

It is a process of heating substances at a high temperature and the resultant conversion of metals into their oxides.

Calcium [Ca]

It is the fifth most abundant element, with atomic number 20. This relatively soft, grey-coloured alkaline earth metal is used as a reducing agent, alloying agent, etc.

Calcium carbonate [$CaCO_3$]

Occurring naturally in limestone and marble, it is a colourless, indissoluble solid used for manufacturing paints, rubber tires, etc.

Calcium chloride [$CaCl_2$]

This white, crystalline salt of calcium and chlorine is used as a drying agent, and also for defrosting purposes.

Calcium fluoride [CaF_2]

Occurring naturally as the mineral fluorite, this ionic, insoluble solid is used as a window material, flux, etc.

Calcium hydroxide [$Ca(OH)_2$]

Another name for hydrated lime, it is a white powder, which is used as a cleaning agent in sewage treatment, and is used in paper and food industry as well.

Calcium nitrate [$Ca(NO_3)_2$]

This colourless, deliquescent, water-soluble salt, also called Norgessalpeter, is chiefly used as a constituent in fertilizers.

Calcium oxide [CaO]

Usually known as quicklime or burnt lime, it is a colourless, caustic and alkaline crystalline solid at room temperature, and is mainly used for producing calcium hydroxide.

Calcium phosphate [$Ca_3(PO_4)_2$]

This calcium salt or phosphoric acid (or of several similar acids) is the main component of bones, and is chiefly used for producing phosphoric acid and fertilizers.

Californium [Cf]

A synthetic, transuranic, radioactive metallic element in the actinide series, with atomic number 9, is used mainly as a neutron emitter.

Calixarene

It is a macrocyclic structure comprising the group $(ArCH_2)_n$, whereAr is aryl group.

Calomel half cell

Also known as calomel electrode, it is a reference electrode containing mercury, mercurous chloride and potassium chloride, and is used in electrometric measurement of acidity, voltammetry, etc.

Calorimeter

It is a device used to assess the heat transfer between systems and surroundings.

Camphor [$C_{10}H_{16}O$]

Occurring naturally in trees and essential oils, it is a colourless, volatile, fragrant, crystalline substance used in food, medicines, etc.

Cane sugar

It is sucrose (carbohydrate comprising glucose and fructose) derived from sugarcane.

Cannabinoids

It is a group of closely related compounds, which include cannabinol and the active components of cannabis.

Cannizzaro reaction

It is a chemical reaction involving an aldehyde's base-induced disproportionation.

Capillary

It is a tube with a small inside diameter.

Capillary action

It is the drawing a liquid inside a small-bore tube when adhesive forces are greater than cohesive forces.

Capillary electrophoresis

Also called capillary zone electrophoresis, it is a separation process based on the differential electrophoretic migration rate of sample components when a voltage is applied in the interior of a capillary.

Capric acid [$CH_3(CH_2)_8COOH$]

Another name of decanoic acid, it is a saturated fatty acid with an unpleasant odour and is obtained from animal oils and fats. It is used in perfumes, flavours, etc.

Caprolactam [$(CH_2)_5C(O)NH$]

This colourless, synthetic, crystalline solid, which is a cyclic amide of caproic acid, is used in the manufacture of nylon (polyamide).

Caprylic acid

Also called octanoic acid, it is a liquid fatty acid with a sour taste which occurs naturally and is present in butter and other fats.

Carbanion

It is an organic ion bearing a negative charge on a carbon atom.

Carbazole

Obtained from coal tar, this aromatic, colourless crystalline substance is used in manufacturing dyes.

Carbene

It is an extremely reactive molecule, which contains a bivalent carbon atom with two non-bonding valence electrons.

Carbide

It is a binary compound made of carbon and an element of lower electronegativity.

Carbocation

Also known as carbonium and carbenium ion, these are ions with a positively-charged carbon atom.

Carbolic acid

Also known as phenol, it is a poisonous, colourless, soluble, crystalline substance, derived from benzene, and is used for making disinfectants.

Carbon

With atomic number 6, this abundant non-metallic tetravalent element occurs in all organic compounds. It has two primary forms, diamond and graphite; and charcoal, soot and coal are other impure forms.

Carbonate

Formed by the reaction of carbon dioxide with bases, carbonate is a salt or ester of the anion CO_3^{2-}.

Carbon black

Produced by burning hydrocarbons in insufficient air, it is a black colloidal substance which consists of amorphous carbon, and isused mainly as a pigment.

Carbon dioxide [CO_2]

Produced by burning carbon, organic compounds, and by respiration, this colourless, odourless gas is present in air, and is used in food, beverages, etc.

Carbonic acid [H_2CO_3]

When carbon dioxide combines with water, this weak acid known only in solution is produced.

Carbon monoxide [CO]

Also known as carbonic oxide, it is a colourless, odourless, poisonous, inflammable gas. Formed by incomplete combustion of carbon, this gas is used in the chemical and pharmaceutical industry.

Carbonyl group

This is a functional group made of a carbon atom double-bonded to an oxygen atom.

Carboxyl group

This functional COOH group is found within carboxyl acids.

Carbyne

Occurring as a short-lived reactive intermediate, carbyne is a monovalent carbon radical species, in which there is a chain of carbon atoms with alternating single and triple bonds.

Carcinogen

It is any substance radionuclide or radiation that is an agent directly involved in causing cancer in humans and animals.

Carius method

This method involves heating the sample to analyze and examine organic compounds for sulphur, halogens and phosphorus.

Caro's acid [H_2SO_5]

Also known as persulphuric acid, peroxysulfuric acid and peroxymonosulfuric acid, this disulphuric and highly explosive acid (liquid at room temperature) is used as a disinfectant.

Casein

This protein is commonly found in mammalian milk. It is used in processed cheese, as food additives and also as adhesives, etc.

Cast iron

It is an alloy of iron and carbon, which has more carbon than iron. This hard, heavy, brittle, unchangeable metal is formed by casting in molds, mostly used for architectural purposes.

Catalysis

It is the acceleration of a reaction caused by the presence of a substance that remains chemically unchanged when the reaction has ended.

Catalyst

It is a substance that causes or accelerates the rate at which a chemical reaction takes place.

Catechol[$C_6H_4(OH)_2$]

Another name for pyrocatechol, this colourless, organic compound is used as an astringent and in photography, etc.

Catenane

It is a mechanically-interlocked molecular structures of two or more interlocked macrocycles. It simple means a type of chemical compound in which the moleucles have two or more rings that are interlocked like the links of a chain.

Catenation

It is the bonding together of atoms of the same element to form chains.

Cathode

It is an electrode through which electric current flows out of an electric device.

Cathode ray tube

It is a closed glass tube filled within ert gas, and produces cathode rays when high voltage is applied.

Cation

It is (i) a positive ion that is attracted to the cathode in elctrolysis; (ii) any positively charged atom or group of atoms.

Caustic soda

Another name for sodium hydroxide (NaOH), this strong alkaline substance is used for making paints, detergents, etc.

Cell

It is a device that has electrodes immersed in an electrolyte utilized for producing electric current.

Cellulose

This indissoluble substance, which is a component of plant tissues and vegetable fibers, is a polysaccharide comprising chains of glucose monomers.

Cementation

This process involves the impregnation (part of plastination) of the surface of a metal with another material by means of high-temperature diffusion.

Central atom

It is (i) an atom in a molecule; (ii) a polyatomic ion that is bonded to more than one other atom.

Cerium [Ce]

This silvery-white, ductile metallic element, with atomic number 58, is from the lanthanide series of elements, and is used mainly as a catalytic converter.

Cetane

This hydrocarbon of the alkane series, also known as hexadecane ($C_{16}H_{34}$), is a colourless liquid of petrochemical derivative.

Chain

It is a part of a molecule comprising a number of atoms linked together in a linear order.

Chain reaction

This reaction, in which reactive species are produced in more than one step, when started, sustains itself and expands.

Chair confirmation

This stable chemical conformation is the spatial arrangement of atoms in a cyclical manner (a six-membered ring).

Charcoal

It is formed when an organic matter (wood, bone, etc.) is heated in the absence of air. This residual, porous, black solid is used as fuel, for purification, in medicine, etc.

Charge-transfer complex

Another name for electron-donor-acceptor complex, it is an association of molecules, in which electronic charge is transferred between the molecules.

Charle's law

This law states that at constant pressure, the volume occupied by a definite mass of gas is directly proportionate to its absolute temperature.

Chemical bond

It is an attraction which holds atoms together in elements or compounds. The bond takes place by the electrostatic force that causes attraction between opposite charges between electrons and nuclei, or dipole attraction.

Chemical dating

It is a technique in which measuring the chemical compositions helps to ascertain the age of minerals (relative or absolute) and of ancient objects.

Chemical equation

It symbolically describes a chemical reaction in which the formulas of the reactants are on the left of an arrow and the formulas of products are on the right.

Chemical equilibrium

It is a state of dynamic balance in which the rates of forward and reverse reactions are equal.

Chemical reaction

It is a phenomenon that involves the creation or division of chemical bonds and results in the transformation of one set of chemical substances to another.

Chirality

It implies a phenomenon in which an object varies from its mirror image, having different left-handed and right-handed forms.

Chloral [Cl_3CCHO]

Also called trichloroacetaldehyde, this aldehyde is a colourless, thick and oily liquid. This organic compound, prepared by chlorinating acetaldehyde, is used in the preparation of DDT (insecticide).

Chlorates

These are (i) the salts of chloric acid with the anion ClO_3^-; (ii) chemical compounds having this anion.

Chloric acid [$HClO_3$]

Found in chlorate salts, this colourless, strong, unstable, liquid acid with a pungent smell has strong oxidising properties.

Chloride

It is a compound of chlorine with a salt of the anion Cl^-.

Chlorine

Commonly known as a heavy, poisonous, yellow-green-coloured gas, this non-metallic element with atomic number 17 is used as a bleaching agent, and also for purification of water.

Chlorite

It is a salt of chlorous acid, having the anion ClO_2^-.

Chlorobenzene [C_6H_5Cl]

Made from chlorine and benzene, this colourless, aromatic and inflammable liquid is used as a solvent, and as an intermediate for making chemicals.

Chlorofluorocarbon

Commonly known as CFC, it is a group of compounds containing carbon, hydrogen, chlorine, and fluorine. Known for damaging the ozone layer, these gases are used mainly in refrigerants and aerosol propellants.

Chromate

It is any salt or ester of chromic acid, in which the anion has both chromium and oxygen.

Chromatogram

It is a record displaying the result of separation of the constituents of a mixture by chromatography.

Chrome alum [$KCr(SO_4)_2 \cdot 12\ (H_2O)$]

This violet-coloured, crystalline salt (compound) is utilized in photographic processing and dyeing.

Chrome red

It is a red pigment, which has lead chromate and lead oxide.

Chrome yellow

It is a yellow pigment consisting of lead chromate.

Chromic acid [H_2CrO_4]

An unstable, corrosive, strongly oxidizing acid, which exists only in the form of solution and as chromate salts, and is used in ceramic glazes, glasses, etc.

Chromium [Cr]

It is a hard, brittle, multivalent, white metallic element, with atomic number 24. This metal being resistant to corrosion is used in stainless steel and other alloys, for chromium plating, and for various other uses.

Chromyl chloride [CrO_2Cl_2]

This highly electrophilic and aggressively oxidizing chemical compound is an opaque dark red liquid at room temperature and pressure.

Cinnamic acid [$C_6H_5CHCHCOOH$]

Found in basalms, this colourless, aromatic, mildly water-soluble crystalline acid is used in medicines, flavours, etc.

Citric acid [$C_6H_8O_7$]

This pungent-tasting, crystalline acid found in the juice of sour fruits (lemon) serves as a natural preservative. It is used as flavouring agent in food, as a cleaning agent, etc.

Clay

It is a group of silicate and aluminosilicate minerals with sheet-like structures that can absorb huge amounts of water.

Coacervate

It is a small sphere-shaped droplet of various organic molecules, which is kept intact by hydrophobic forces from a surrounding liquid.

Coagulation

It is (i) the conversion from a liquid to a semisolid state; (ii) the precipitation of suspended colloidal particles by the means of physical or chemical processes.

Cobalt [Co]

The lusturous, hard, magnetic, light-grey metallic element with atomic number 27 is used in alloys, batteries, etc.

Coke

Obtained by destructive distillation of coal or petroleum, this solid, residual, impure form of carbon is used in blast furnaces and also as a fuel.

Colchicine

Extracted from plants of the genus Colchicum, this poisonous natural product and secondary metabolite has a wide usage in the pharmaceutical industry.

Collagen

It is a class of natural proteins, found in animals, especially in the flesh, connective tissues, and fibrous tissues (tendons, ligaments and skin) of mammals. It is used in food and industry as gelatin, a collagen which is irreversibly hydrolyzed.

Colligative properties

These are physical properties of solutions that depend upon the number of solute particles present.

Collision theory

This theory of reaction rates implies that effective collisions between reactant molecules must take place in order for reaction to take place.

Collodion

This colourless, flammable, syrupy solution of nitrocellulose in a mixture of alcohol and ether is utilized chiefly in surgery (coating on wounds).

Colloids

It is a heterogeneous mixture in which solute-like particles are in a suspended state.

Combination reaction

It is a reaction in which two substances combine to form a single substance known as a compound.

Combinatorial chemistry

It is a technique for performing a large number of reactions at the same time on a small scale to produce a library of linked compounds.

Combustion

It is the swift chemical combination of a substance with oxygen resulting in the generation of heat and light.

Complex ions

These ions are the outcome of the formation of coordinate covalent bonds between simple ions and other ions. They are soluble in solutions.

Component

It is (i) a part of the mixture; (ii) a particular chemical species in a mixture.

Compound

It is a substance composed of two or more elements in fixed proportions.

Computational chemistry

This chemistry makes use of principles of computer science to help in computing and resolving chemical problems.

Concentration

It is the amount of solute per unit volume.

Concerted reaction

It is a chemical reaction in which all bonds are made and broken in a single step.

Condensation

It is the change of water from its gaseous form, that is, water vapour into liquid water. In short, it is the liquefaction of vapour.

Condensation reaction

It is a chemical reaction in which two molecules combine to form one single molecule with the elimination of a small molecule.

Conductiometric titration

It is titration based on monitoring the alterations in the electrical conductance of a reaction mixture as one reactant is added.

Configuration

It is the fixed arrangement of the atoms in a molecule by the chemical bonding. It cannot be altered without breaking the bond.

Conformations

These are spatial arrangement of atoms in a molecule that can come about through free rotation of the atoms about a single bond.

Conformational analysis

It is the estimation of the spatial arrangement of the constituent atoms or a group of atoms in a molecule and the way in which this influences chemical behaviour.

Congeners

These are related chemicals such as elements in the same group of the periodic table.

Conjugate acid-base pair

In Bronsted-Lowry terminology, a reactant and product that differ by a proton, HX.

Contact process

It is an industrial process by which sulphur trioxide and sulphuric acid are formed from sulphur dioxide.

Continuous spectrum

It has all wave lengths in a specified region of the electromagnetic spectrum.

Coordinate covalent bond

It is a covalent bond in which both shared electrons are furnished by the same bond.

Coordination compound

It is a compound that has coordinate covalent bonds.

Copolymer

It consists of two or more different monomeric species.

Copper [Cu]

This ductile, red-brown, corrosion-resistant, diamagnetic metallic element of atomic number 29 serves as an electrical and thermal conductor.

Coprecipitation

It is the precipitation of more than one substance at the same time.

Corrosion

It is the oxidation of metals in the presence of air and moisture.

Coulomb

It is a unit of electrical charge.

Coumarin [$C_9H_6O_2$]

Found in many plants (tonka bean, vanilla grass, etc.), this colourless, crystalline, vanilla-scented compound is used for making medicines, perfumes, etc.

Counter ion

These are anions (cations) in a coordination compound that balance the charge on the complex ion.

Cresols

Synonymous with methylphenols, these are any of three isomeric phenols, $CH_3C_6H_4OH$, and are used as disinfectants and deodorisers.

Critical point

It is combining of critical temperature and critical pressure of a substance.

Critical state

It is the state when the substance is at its critical point (at critical temperature, volume and pressure above which they do not exist).

Critical temperature

It is the temperature of a gas in its critical state.

Crown ethers

These are cyclic chemical compounds that consists of a ring having a number of ether groups.

Crystal

It is a solid comprising a symmetrical, arranged, three-dimensional collection of atoms or molecules.

Crystalline

It is something which relates to the nature of crystals, with a three-dimensional molecular structure.

Cubane [C_8H_8]

This synthetic, solid, crystalline substance (hydrocarbon molecule) has the carbon atoms placed at the vertices of a cube.

Curare

Found in the bark and stems of some South American plants, this toxic, bitter, resinous substance (alkaloid) serves as a muscle relaxant used in anesthesia.

Curium

Produced artificially by bombarding plutonium with helium nuclei, this synthetic radioactive, transuranic, metallic element, with atomic number 96, is used in space exploration.

Cyanamide

It is (i) a weak, soluble, acidic crystalline compound; (ii) a salt of this having the anion CN_2^{2-}.

Cyanide

It is an extremely toxic salt of hydrocyanic acid, which has the anion CN^-.

Cyanogen

This pseudohalogen, produced by oxidizing hydrogen cyanide, is a colourless, flammable, toxic gas with an acrid smell.

Cyclamates

Used as artificial sweeteners, these are calcium or sodium salts of cyclohexanesulphamic acid.

Cyclisation

It is a phenomenon which leads to the alteration from an open-chain to the formation of a closed ring.

Cyclobutadiene [C_4H_4]

Also called butene, this is the smallest annulene, with the shortest life highly unstable and extremely reactive hydrocarbon.

Cyclohexane [C_6H_{12}]

This cycloalkane, derived from petroleum, is a colourless, volatile liquid, used mainly in the chemical industry.

Cyclonite

Commonly known as RDX, it is a colourless, crystalline, explosive nitroamine, used in military operations and for industrial uses.

Cyclopropane

This cycloalkane molecule is a colourless, flammable gas used as an anesthetic.

❑

Dalton's atomic theory

Named after the English chemist, John Dalton, this modern atomic theory states that (i) elements are made of atoms (particles); (ii) atoms cannot be produced, subdivided, or destructed; (iii) atoms of different elements combine to form compounds.

Daniell cell

Invented by John Daniell, it is an electrochemical cell in which a reaction takes place between zinc and aqueous copper ions.

Daughter nuclide

This nuclide is generated in a nuclear decay.

D-block elements

Also known as transition elements, these occupy that part of the periodic table that includes only Groups 3-11.

DDT

This chlorinated hydrocarbon, also called dichlorodiphenyltrichloroethane, is a synthetic organic compound which is chiefly used as an insecticide.

Deactivation

It means disrupting of chemical activity by deactivating a catalyst or an enzyme.

Deamination

This implies removing an amino group from an amino acid or compound.

Debye

It is the unit used to denote dipole moments.

Debye-Huckel theory

This theory in physical chemistry explains the deviation from ideality in solutions of electrolytes because of the electrical forces between ions.

Decahydrate

It is a crystalline hydrate whose solid contains ten molecules of water per unit cell.

Decarboxylation

It is the phenomenon in which a carboxyl group is removed from a chemical compound.

Decomposition

It is the reverse of chemical synthesis, in which a chemical compound is broken into elements or simpler compounds.

Deflagration

It is the act of burning that propagates through thermal conductivity at subsonic speeds.

Degradation

It means simplification of a chemical by breaking it down into simpler compounds.

Degrees of freedom

This term conveys the dependence on parameters, and suggests the potentiality of counting the number of those parameters.

Dehydration

It is described as a state which involves the loss of water from a substance (or molecule).

Dehydrogenation

It is a chemical process involving the elimination of hydrogen from a compound.

Dehydrohalogenation

This elimination reaction involves the elimination of a hydrogen atom and a halogen atom from a compound.

Deliquescence

It is a phenomenon in which a hygroscopic substance takes in moisture from the atmosphere till it dissolves in the concentrated solution.

Delocalisation

Related to electrons, it refers to bonding electrons that are spread among more than two atoms that are bonded together.

Denaturation

It is a phenomenon concerning a change in structure of a protein from regular to irregular arrangement of the polypeptide chains.

Dendrimers

These polymers are spherical-shaped, tree-like branched molecules.

Denitrification

It is a process in which nitrates are broken down by the bacteria in the soil resulting in the harmless atmospheric nitrogen gas.

Density

D=MV: denoting the mass of a substance per unit of volume.

Depolarisation

It means a loss of polarity.

Depsides

Mostly found in lichens, it is a group of intermolecular esters (compounds) made from phenolic benzoic acids.

Derivative

It is a compound that arises from a parent compound by replacement of one atom with a group of atoms.

Desiccant

This hygroscopic substance (calcium chloride, lime, etc.) is used as a drying agent because of its high affinity to water.

Desorption

It is the removal of an adsorbed substance from the surface of a solid adsorbent.

Destructive distillation

It is a chemical process in which organic material is heated in the absence of air. The destructive distillation of coal results in the formation of products like coke, coal gas, coal tar, etc.

Detergent

It is a soap-like emulsifier that has a sulphate SO_3, or a phosphate group instead of a carboxylate group.

Deuterium [D]

It is an isotope of hydrogen whose atoms have both a proton and a neutron in the nucleus.

Deuterium oxide

Another name for heavy water, it is the water having a substantial proportion of deuterium atoms.

Devitrification

It means to deprive of glassy lustre and transparency as the molecules in the glass transform their structure into that of crystalline solids.

Dewar structure

It is an aromatic structure for benzene that contains a bond between opposite atoms.

Dialysis

It is the breaking up of particles in a liquid by means of their unequal diffusion in passing through a semipermeable membrane.

Diamagnetism

A property of certain materials of being reppled by both magnetic poles. It is the weak repulsion by a magnetic field. Substances like water that are generally considered non-magnetic are actually diamagnetic.

Diamond

Known as the hardest substance found in nature, this clear, colourless, crystalline form of pure carbon is used as a semi-conductor, gemstone, etc.

Diastereoisomers

Also called diastereomers, these are stereoisomers that are not related as mirror images.

Diatomic molecule

It is a molecule having only two atoms of either the same or different chemical element.

Diazotisation

Also called diazo process, it is the conversion of an amine into a diazo compound.

Dibasic acid

It is an acid that has two acidic hydrogen atoms per molecule.

Dicarboxylic acid

Any carboxylic acid that contains two carboxylic groups per molecule.

Dichlorobenzene

This includes three compounds: (i) ortho-dichlorobenzene, (ii) meta-dichlorobenzene, and (iii) para-dichlorobenzene.

Diels-Alder reaction

It is an organic chemical reaction in which bicyclic molecules and rings are formed by the combination of adiene (conjugated) and a dienophile (substituted alkene).

Diene

This unsaturated hydrocarbon or organic compound has two double bonds between carbon atoms.

Dienophile

It is a substituted alkene which readily reacts with diene.

Diethanolamine

Commonly known as DEA, this colourless, water-soluble, hygroscopic liquid is used as a chemical intermediate, corrosion inhibitor, etc.

Diethyl ether

Also called ethoxyethane, this colourless, volatile liquid with a peculiar smell is used as a fuel, solvent, etc.

Differential thermal analysis

Abbreviated as DTA, it is a method for observing the temperature, direction, and magnitude of thermally induced transitions in a substance.

Diffusion

It is a process in which the substances intermingle by the natural movement of their particles (going from high to low concentration).

Dihydrate

It is a crystalline hydrate that has two molecules of water of crystallization per molecule.

Dilatancy

It is a phenomenon in which some fluids become thicker under pressure.

Diluent

It is a substance used to dilute something such as a diluting agent.

Dilute

It is thinning the concentration of a solution by adding another solvent to it.

Dimer

It is a chemical substance consisting of two structurally similar monomers bound together by either weak or strong bonds. This molecule is formed by combining two identical molecules.

Dimethylbenzene

Synonymous with xylene, it includes three colourless, pleasant-smelling hydrocarbon liquids, where each has two methyl groups substituted on the benzene ring.

Dimorphism

It is the property of some substances where they exist in two distinct forms.

Dinitrogen

It is when the nitrogen molecule contains two atoms, or is diatomic.

Dioxin

It is a heterocyclic, antiaromatic, carcinogenic, toxic compound.

Dioxygen

It is the normal form of molecular oxygen.

Diphenylamine $[(C_6H_5)_2NH]$

It is a colourless, synthetic, crystalline solid, used in the production of dyes, medicines, explosives, etc.

Diphosgene

This colourless liquid is widely used as a reagent in the synthesis of organic compounds.

Dipole

It describes the separation of charge between two atoms bonded in a covalent manner.

Dipole-dipole interactions

These are attractive interactions between polar molecules.

Diquat

This contact herbicide is a synthetic compound used for inhibiting plant growth.

Disperse phase

Also called discontinuous phase, it is the solute-like species in a colloid.

Disproportionation

These are redox reactions in which the compound is oxidized and reduced at the same time.

Dissociation

It is a process in which a solid ionic compound separates into its ions usually in a reversible manner.

Distillation

It is the process in which components of a mixture are separated by boiling the liquid, condensing and collecting the liquid.

Distilled water

It is the water from which the impurities have been removed using distillation.

Dithionate

It is a salt of dithionic acid.

Dithionic acid [$H_2S_2O_6$]

This chemical compound is dibasic and only dithionates (salts) are known.

Donnan equilibrium

Also known as Gibbs-Donnan equilibrium, this is the equilibrium attained between two ionic solutions divided by a membrane when one or more of the types of ion present are not able to pass through the semipermeable membrane.

Double decomposition

Also called metathesis, it is a chemical reaction between two compounds in which radicals of both are exchanged to form two new compounds.

Double salt

It is a solid that consists of two co-crystallized salts.

Doublet

It is pair of two peaks or bands of about equal intensity appearing close together on a spectrogram.

Dry cell

These are ordinary batteries (voltaic cells) in which the electrolyte is in the form of a paste preventing it from flowing.

Dubnium [Db]

Produced by high-energy atomic collisions, it is an unstable, transuranic, synthetic, radioactive element with atomic number 105.

Dumas' method

It is a method used to determine (i) the molecular weights of volatile liquids; (ii) the amount of nitrogen in chemical substances.

Dyes

Also called dyestuff, it is a natural or synthetic substance, which is used to colour other materials.

❑

Echelon grating

It is a diffraction grating comprising a stack of equally thick glass plates placed stepwise with a constant offset.

Effective collisions

These are collisions between molecules resulting in a reaction.

Effective nuclear charge

It is the nuclear charge experienced by the outermost electrons of an atom.

Effervescence

It is the forming of gas bubbles in an aqueous solution creating fizz when the gas is released.

Effusion

It is the process in which there is a flow of gas molecules through a small opening without collisions between molecules.

Einstein equation

Also known as mass-energy equivalence, $E = mc^2$, it is the principle that a measured quantity of mass is equal to a measured quantity of energy.

Einsteinium [Es]

Created by bombarding plutonium with neutrons, it is a radioactive, transuranic, synthetic element of the actinide series, with atomic number 99.

Electrical conductivity

It is the ability of a material to conduct electricity.

Electrochemical cell

This device consists of an anode and a cathode in metallic contact and immersed in an electrolyte, which either draws electrical energy from reactions or produces reactions through electrical energy.

Electrochemical equivalent

It is the weight of a substance that is accumulated at an electrode when one coulomb of electricity charge is passed.

Electrochemistry

It is the study of chemical action generated by electrical current and the creation of electricity by chemical reactions.

Electrocyclic reaction

It is a kind of pericyclic reaction in which the outcome is the conversion from one pi bond into one sigma bond or one sigma bond to one pi bond.

Electrode

It is a conductor through which electricity comes in or goes out of a substance.

Electrode potential

It is the potential difference between the charge on an electrode and in the solution.

Electrodialysis

It is a method in which electrical current is applied to permeable membranes for the removal of charged particles from water.

Electrolysis

This phenomenon that takes place in electrolytic cells is a chemical decomposition reaction generated by passing electric current through a solution having ions.

Electrolyte

It is a substance whose aqueous solutions containing positive or negative ions conduct electricity.

Electrolytic cell

It is a cell in which chemical reactions take place when an outside source of electrical energy is applied.

Electrolytic conduction

It is the conduction of electrical current by the movement of ions through a pure liquid.

Electromagnetic radiation

It is the wave-like form of energy that is transmitted by means of electric and magnetic fields, which vary at the same time.

Electromotive force

Commonly known as emf, it is the difference in potential that tends to develop an electric current (electrons, ions).

Electromotive series

Another name for activity series, it is the relative order of elements or ions in order of their electrode potentials ascertained under specified circumstances.

Electron

It is one of the three atomic particles, which has a negative elementary electric charge (–1).

Electron affinity

It is the amount of energy released in the process in which an electron is added to a neutral gaseous atom to form a negative ion (–1).

Electronegativity

A measure of the relative tendency of an atom to attract electrons to itself when chemically combined with another atom.

Electron flow

It is an electric current generated by the movement of electrons from negative to a positive terminal.

Electronic transition

It is the transfer of a valence electron from one energy level to a higher energy level.

Electroosmosis

Formerly called electroendosmosis, it is the flow of liquid induced by an applied potential across a porous material, cappilary tube, membrane, etc.

Electrophile

It is an ion or molecule which is positively charged or is electron-deficient.

Electrophoresis

Synonymous with cataphoresis, it is a method for separating charged particles in a colloid in an electric field.

Electrophoretic effect

This trend of the applied potential to move the ionic atmosphere itself slows down the movement of ions within a solution.

Electroplating

It is the process of plating a metal onto a surface with the use of electrical current.

Electropositive

It pertains to elements which lose electrons and form positive ions in chemical reactions.

Electrovalent bond

Also called ionic bond, it is a chemical bond that takes place between two oppositely charged ions.

Element

A chemical element is a substance made of atoms which cannot be broken down into simpler forms. There are 92 elements which are naturally found.

Elementary reaction

Also called step, it is a reaction in which the chemical species react immediately without intermediates to form products with a single transition state.

Elimination reaction

This intramolecular substitution occurs when a molecule loses atoms or groups of atoms resulting in a new bond.

Eluent

It is the solvent used in the process of elution for separating materials.

Elution

It is a method of separating materials by extraction by washing with a solvent.

Emission spectrum

It is a spectrum related to emission of electromagnetic radiation by atoms due to electronic transitions from higher to ground energy levels.

Empirical formula

It is the formula of a substance or chemical compound, where relative numbers of atoms of each element are shown.

Emulsification

It is the phenomenon by which an emulsion is formed by blending two or more unmixable liquids.

Emulsion

It is the colloidal suspension in which both phases are liquids.

Enantiomer

It is one of the two mirror-image forms of an optically active molecule.

Enantiomorphism

It is the relationship demonstrated by a pair of enantiomorphs (compounds that are non-superimposable mirror images of each other).

Endo

This prefix denotes a special type of isomerism occurring in compounds with a substituent on a bridged ring system.

Endothermic

It refers to chemical reactions that absorb heat energy from its surroundings.

End point

It is the point at which a titration stops as the indicator changes colour.

Energy

It is the ability to do work or transfer heat.

Enols

These are compounds which consist of a hydroxyl group bonded to carbon atoms containing the double bond.

Enthalpy

It is the heat content of a specific amount of substance.

Entropy

It is a thermodynamic property that is a measure of the degree of disorder of a system.

Enzyme

It is a protein naturally occurring in the living organism that acts as a catalyst in particular biological reactions.

Epoxides

These are compounds whose molecule has a three-membered ring.

Epoxyethane [C_2H_4O]

Also known as ethylene oxide, this simplest epoxide is a colourless, inflammable gas with a mild fragrance.

Epoxy resin

Produced by the polymerisation of an epoxide, it is a thermosetting polymer used in adhesives, laminates, etc.

Equation of state

It describes the behaviour of matter in a given state.

Equilibrium

It is a state of dynamic balance in which no changes take place and the rates of forward and reverse reactions are equal.

Equilibrium constant

It is the value that shows how long the reaction goes on until equilibrium is reached.

Equivalence point

It is the point in a titration at which the equivalent amounts of reactants have reacted and solution is completely neutral.

Erbium [Er]

With atomic number 68, this soft, silvery-white trivalent metallic element of the lanthanide series is used in laser applications.

Esterification

It is a chemical reaction of an alcohol with an acid to formester.

Esters

Derived by reaction between an acid and an alcohol, with removal of water, these organic compounds are used in perfumes, plastics, flavourings, etc.

Ethane [C_2H_6]

This constituent of petroleum and natural gas is a colourless, odourless, volatile gas which is used primarily in the chemical industry.

Ethanol

Also known as ethyl alcohol, this inflammable, clear, colourless liquid is mostly found in alcoholic drinks as an intoxicating agent and is also used as fuel.

Ethene [C_2H_4]

Made from petroleum and natural gas, this inflammable colourless gaseous alkene with a mild fragrance, also called ethylene, is used in the chemical industry.

Ethers

Another name for ethyl ether, it is an aromatic, flammable, colourless, volatile liquid used as a solvent and intermediate.

Ethylamine [$CH_3CH_2NH_2$]

This colourless, volatile liquid amine with a strong smell is widely used for industrial purposes and organic synthesis.

Ethylbenzene [$C_6H_5CH_2CH_3$]

A colourless, flammable liquid with a gasoline-like smell is used to make styrene, and is also used as a solvent.

Ethyl bromide [C_2H_5Br]

This volatile compound with an ether-like smell, also called bromoethane. It is used in organic synthesis.

Ethyne [C_2H_2]

This simplest alkyne, also called acetylene, is a colourless, flammable gas used mainly in organic synthesis.

Europium [Eu]

This trivalent soft silvery-white metallic element of the lanthanide series with atomic number 63 is used in television sets, fluorescent lamps, etc.

Eutectic mixture

Also called eutectic system, it is a mixture of substances or chemical compounds which have a melting point lower than that of any of its constituents.

Evaporation

It is the conversion of a liquid to the gaseous state (vapour).

Exothermic

It describes chemical reactions which release heat energy.

Extender

It is a material added to a product to dilute its colour or add to its bulk.

Extraction

It is the technique of deriving a component from a mixture by chemical means.

Extrapolate

It is an estimation of the value of a result outside the range of a series of known values.

❑

Fahrenheit scale

On this temperature scale, the freezing point of water is 32°F and the boiling point is 212°F.

Fatty acid

It is a carboxylic acid with an unbranched aliphatic chain, which can be saturated or unsaturated. Most of these occur naturally and can also be obtained from fat by hydrolysis.

Fermentation

It is a phenomenon in which an agent (yeast, bacteria) breaks down an organic substance into simpler forms.

Fermium [Fm]

Derived artificially by bombarding plutonium with neutrons, it is a radioactive, synthetic, transuranic metallic element of the actinide series, with atomic number 100.

Ferrate

It is a salt in which the anion contains both iron and oxygen.

Ferric compounds [Fe^{3+}]

These iron-containing materials with an oxidation number of +3, denoted as iron (III), are the most stable form of iron in air.

Ferricyanide

Produced by oxidation of a ferrocyanide, it is a salt having the anion $Fe(CN)_6^{3-}$, which is used in the organic industry.

Ferrite

This unstable, magnetic, ceramic compound with iron (III) oxide (Fe_2O_3) is used in making antennas, transformers, etc.

Ferrocene [$Fe(C_5H_5)_2$]

It is an orange-coloured, crystalline, organometallic compound with its molecules having a sandwich structure.

Ferrocyanide

Produced by a reaction of a cyanide with iron sulphate, this salt of ferrocyanic acid contains the anion Fe $(CN)_6^{4-}$.

Ferromagnetism

It is the ability of a substance to become permanently magnetised in a magnetic field.

Ferrous compounds [Fe^{2+}]

These are iron-containing materials with oxidation number of +2, denoted as iron (II).

Fertilizer

This is a substance used to increase soil's fertility and improve plant growth.

Film badge

It is a patch of photographic film worn to monitor accumulated ionising radiation.

Filter

It is a porous apparatus for eliminating impurities or particles from a liquid or gas.

Filtration

It is the process of filtering in which there is a separation of solids from fluids.

Fischer projection

It is a projection in which a three-dimensional organic molecule is represented in a two-dimensional way.

Fittig reaction

Also known as Wurtz reaction, it involves the alkylation of aryl halides.

Flame

It is a hot glowing body of ignited gas that is produced by combustion.

Flash photolysis

It is a technique of examining fast photochemical reactions in gases.

Flash point

It is the lowest temperature at which the vapour above liquid will produce an inflammable mixture with air.

Flocculation

It is the process of flocculating in which colloids are no longer in suspension, forming an aggregated fluffy mass.

Flocculent

It is a material that has a fluffy or cloud-like character.

Flotation

It is a process by which water-repelling particles of an ore are separated from water-attracting particles.

Fluorescein

This fluorophore is an orange/redpowder with a yellowish-green fluorescence, soluable in water and is used as an indicator, in medicines, etc.

Fluorescence

It is the taking in of high energy radiation by a substance and resultant emission of visible light.

Fluoride

This monovalent ion and a salt of hydrofluoric acid is used to prevent tooth decay, and also as a reagent.

Fluorination

It is a chemical reaction in which the fluorine atom is introduced into a compound.

Fluorine [F]

It is a non-metallic, univalent, highly reactive element of the halogen series with atomic number 9. This inflammable, toxic, pale-yellow gas is used in steel-making, aluminium refining, etc.

Fluorocarbons

Another name for fluorohydrocarbons, it is a compound in which some hydrogen atoms are replaced by fluorine.

Flux

It is a substance added to a solid to lower its melting point, and is used mainly in soldering metals.

Fluxional molecule

This molecule undergoes a dynamic rearrangement of some or all atoms, and has an ever-changing structure.

Foam

It is a mass of small bubbles dispersed in a liquid.

Folic acid

Naturally found in green vegetables, liver, this vitamin of the B complex, also called folacin, is important for cell growth.

Force constant

It refers to the force controlling the relative displacement of the cell nucleus in a molecule.

Formaldehyde [HCHO]

Prepared by oxidising methanol, this simplest aldehyde is a colourless pungent, toxic gas which has many industrial uses.

Formate

Another name for methanoate, it is a salt or ester of formic acid.

Formic acid [HCOOH]

Also called methanoic acid, this simplest carboxylic acid occurs naturally. This colourless, pungent liquid is used as a disinfectant, chemical intermediate, etc.

Formula weight

It is the mass of one formula unit of a substance in atomic mass units.

Formyl group

It is a functional group having a carbonyl group joined by a single bond to a hydrogen atom.

Fossil fuels

Obtained from the decomposition of organic materials under geological conditions, these substances (coal, petroleum, natural gas) are carbon or hydrocarbon fuels.

Fractional crystallisation

It is a process of segregating different matters from a solution.

Fractional distillation

It is a method of separating a mixture of substances with small differences in boiling points.

Fractional precipitation

It is a method that segregates ions from solution according to their different solubility.

Francium [Fr]

Found as a disintegration product of actinium, it is a radioactive member of the alkali metal group, with atomic number 87.

Free radical

It is an uncharged molecule with an unpaired valence electron.

Freezing mixture

It is a mixture of substances to get a temperature below 0°C.

Freezing-point depression

It is a colligative property of matter in which there is a decrease in the freezing point of a solvent due to the presence of a solute.

Fuel cell

It is a voltaic cell which converts the chemical energy of a fuel directly into electrical energy.

Functional group

It is a group of atoms representing a potential reaction site in a particular compound.

Furan [C_4H_4O]

It is a colourless, poisonous, volatile, aromatic liquid used in nylon synthesis.

Fusion

Also known as melting, it is the phenomenon of heating a solid substance until it becomes liquid.

❑

Gabriel reaction

It is a reaction in which primary alkyl halides are changed into primary amines with the use of potassium phthalimide.

Gadolinium [Gd]

This soft, ductile, ferromagnetic, silvery-white metallic element of the lanthanide series, with atomic number 64, is used in nuclear reactors for shielding.

Gallic acid [$C_7H_6O_5$]

Derived from tannins, this colourless, crystalline, organic acid is used in producing ink dyes, antioxidants, medicines, etc.

Galvanising

It is applying a thin layer of zinc on a ferrous material to prevent the underlying surface from rusting.

Gamma radiation

It is an electromagnetic radiation with high-energy, short wavelength emitted from an atom's nucleus.

Gangue

It is the impurities (sand, rock, etc.) surrounding the mineral in an ore.

Gas chromatography

This chromatography is used for segregating and examining gases' mixtures.

Gattermann reaction

It is a reaction of hydrocyanic acid with benzene under catalysis.

Geiger counter

It is a counter tube for detecting and measuring ionisin gradiations.

Gel

It is the colloidal suspension of a solid dispersed in a liquid.

Gelatin

Made from collagen, this colourless, tasteless, water-soluble protein is used in the production of glue, jellies, etc.

Gel electrophoresis

It is a method in which a block of gel is used, acting as a screen to segregate molecules.

Gel filtration

It is a technique in which molecules in solution are classified and segregated on the basis of their size.

Geochemistry

It is the study of earth's chemical composition.

Geraniol

This alcohol present in essential oils is an aromatic liquid used in making mosquito repellents, perfumes, etc.

Germanium [Ge]

This shiny, lustrous, hard, greyish-white semi-metallic element, with atomic number 32, is used in optical fibres, electronics, etc.

Getter

It is a reactive substance used for the removal of residual gas from a vacuum system.

Glass electrode

Made of a doped glass membrane, it is a kind of ion-selective electrode (half-cell).

Glauber's salt

It is a white, hydrated sodium sulphate used in the manufacturing of paper, medicine, glass, etc.

Gluconic acid [$C_6H_{12}O_7$]

Obtained by oxidizing glucose, this sugar acid is used as a food additive.

Glucose [$C_6H_{12}O_6$]

It is a simple sugar (monosaccharide) having many forms, and is the principle source of body's energy.

Glycerol

Obtained as a byproduct in soap manufacture, this colourless, syrupy liquid, also called glycerine, is used in the manufacture of explosives, cosmetics, etc.

Glycol

Sometimes called dihydroxy alcohol, it is a compound comprising two hydroxyl (OH) groups.

Glycolic acid [$C_2H_4O_3$]

Another name for hydroxyacetic acid, this colourless, odourless, water-soluble, crystalline solid has several industrial uses, for example, manufacturing pesticides and cosmetics, dyeing textiles, etc.

Gold [Au]

This soft, yellow-coloured, malleable, ductile metallic element of atomic number 79 is used mainly for making jewellery.

Graft copolymer

It is a kind of branched copolymer, where the main chain is structurally different from the side chains.

Graham's law

This law states that the rates of effusion of gases are inversely proportional to the square roots of their densities.

Graphite

This allotropic form of carbon is a grey-coloured, crystalline mineral used in pencils, nuclear reactors, batteries, etc.

Gravimetric analysis

It is an analytical method in which the final quantitative step is the measurement of mass.

Greenhouse effect

It is a phenomenon in which the radiative energy going out of the planet's surface is absorbed by the greenhouse gases, resulting in warming the planet.

Ground state

It is the lowest energy state of an atom or molecule.

Group

It is a vertical column in the periodic table comprising a family of elements.

Gum

It is a water-soluble, sticky secretion by plants, which is used chiefly in making adhesives.

Gunpowder

This explosive containing a powdered mixture of saltpeter, sulphur, and charcoal is used in fuses, fireworks, etc.

Gypsum

Occurring in sedimentary deposits, this white mineral composed of hydrated calcium sulphate is used in making plasters (plaster of Paris), fertilizers, etc.

❑

Haemoglobin

Abbreviated as Hb, it is a protein that transports oxygen in blood.

Hafnium [Hf]

This grey, shiny, lustrous, tetravalent metallic element of the transition series with atomic number 72 is used in filaments and electrodes.

Half cell

Commonly known as an electrode, it is the structure in a voltaic cell in which the oxidation or reduction half-reaction takes place.

Half life

It is the time-period needed for half of a given substance to undergo decay.

Halide

It is a binary compound with one part as halogen atom and the other part from another element or group.

Halo

It is a ring of white or coloured light surrounding a luminous body caused by refraction through ice crystals.

Haloalkanes

Also known as alkyl halides, these are a class of compounds obtained from alkanes having one or more halogens, and are used as refrigerants, solvents, etc.

Halocarbons

These are compounds which mostly consist of carbon and halogen atom, and sometimes hydrogen also.

Haloform reaction

In this chemical reaction, the exhaustive halogenation of a methyl ketone in the presence of a base generates a haloform.

Haloforms

These compounds (CHX_3, where X is a halogen atom) are obtained from methane by substituting three hydrogen atoms for halogen atoms.

Halogenation

In this chemical reaction, a halogen atom is incorporated into a molecule.

Halogens

This series of non-metal elements occupy Group VIIA in the periodic table: fluorine (F), chlorine (Cl), bromine (Br), iodine (I).

Halons

These chemical compounds, derived from hydrocarbons by replacing hydrogen atoms with halogen atoms, are chiefly used in fire extinguishers.

Hard acid

It is a Lewis acid which is difficult to polarize.

Hard base

It is a Lewis base which is difficult to polarize.

Hard water

It is water having calcium and magnesium ions, which makes it difficult for forming lather with soap.

Hassium [Hs]

Produced by atomic collisions, it is an unstable, transuranic, radioactive element with atomic number 108.

Heat of combustion

It is the production of thermal energy when a compound undergoes complete combustion with oxygen.

Heat of condensation

It is the quantity of heat that must be removed from one gram of vapour at its boiling point to condense into a liquid.

Heat of dissociation

It is the amount of heat needed for a given substance to break up into simpler components.

Heat of reaction

Also called the enthalpy of reaction, it is the quantity of heat absorbed or released in a chemical reaction.

Heat of solution

It is the amount of heat evolved or absorbed in the formation of solution that dissolves completely one mole of solute in a large volume of solvent.

Heavy water

It is a colourless liquid containing a heavy isotope of hydrogen (deuterium).

Helicates

Formed by the chemical recognition, these are inorganic, synthetic, helical arrays of molecule.

Helium [He]

This inert, light, colourless gas with atomic number 2 is the lightest member of the noble gas group.

Hemihydrate

It is a crystalline hydrate consisting of one molecule of water per two molecules of the given compound.

Hemiketals

These are compounds obtained from a reaction of a ketone with an alcohol group.

Henry's law

It states that the pressure of the gas above a solution is proportional to the concentration of the gas in the solution.

Heptane

Derived from petroleum, it is a colourless, volatile, inflammable liquid hydrocarbon of the alkane series, which is used as a solvent.

Hetero atom

Any atom that is not carbon or hydrogen is Hetero atom.

Heterogeneous

It denotes a process involving substances in more than two phases.

Heteropolymer

It is a polymer obtained from two or more different kinds of monomer.

Hexachlorobenzene [C_6Cl_6]

Also called perchlorobenzene, this colourless chlorocarbon was formerly used as a fungicide.

Hexyl group

This organic group $CH_3CH_2CH_2CH_2CH_2CH_2$– is obtained from hexane.

Hill reaction

This reaction takes place in photosynthesis, in which there is light-dependent transfer of electrons by chloroplasts.

Hofmann's reaction

Another name for Hofmann rearrangement, it is the change of an acid amide to an amine by treating with bromine and alkali.

Holmium [Ho]

This trivalent, soft, silvery-white metallic element of the lanthanide series, with atomic number 67, is used for medical applications.

Homocyclic

It explains a cyclic system having a closed ring of atoms of the same type.

Homogeneous

This concept relates to the uniformity (composition or character) in a substance.

Homonuclear

These are molecules made of only one kind of element.

Humectant

It is a hygroscopic substance used to preserve moisture levels.

Hybrid orbital

This orbital takes place when two or more atomic orbitals of an isolated atom mix.

Hydrate

It is a crystalline compound which has a definite percentage of water molecules bound to another compound.

Hydrate isomers

These are isomers of crystalline complexes differing in the presence of water inside or outside the coordination sphere.

Hydrazones

Derived by the reaction of hydrazine on ketones or aldehydes, it is a class of organic compounds used in medical biotechnology.

Hydride

It is a binary compound of hydrogen and other elements.

Hydrocarbons

These are organic compounds made entirely of carbon and hydrogen.

Hydrogen [H]

This colourless, light, odourless, inflammable gas, with atomic number 1, is used in the chemical industry.

Hydrogenation

It is the reaction in which hydrogen is added to a carbon-carbon multiple bonds.

Hydrogen bond

It is a dipole-dipole interaction between molecules consisting of hydrogen bonded to an electronegative atom.

Hydrogencarbonate

Synonymous with bicarbonate, it is a salt of carbonic acid (HCO_3^-) in which one hydrogen atom has been replaced.

Hydrolysis

It is the reaction of substance with water or its ions resulting in its breakdown.

Hydrometer

It is an instrument used to measure the densities of liquids.

Hydrophilic

It relates to anything which attracts water.

Hydrophobic

It relates to anything which repels water.

Hydrosol

Obtained by aromatic plants, it is a concentrated, hydrophobic liquid (sol) used in the pharmaceutical industry.

Hydroxide

It is a compound (i) of an oxide and water; (ii) with the hydroxyl group.

Hydroxylation

In this chemical process, a hydroxyl group is introduced into an organic compound.

Hygroscopic

It is the tendency of a substance to absorb water molecules from the environment.

Hyperconjugation

It is a kind of conjugation in which there is a weak interaction between single bonds and conjugated system.

Hyperfine structure

It describes a range of various effects resulting in shifts in the energy levels of atoms or molecules.

❑

Ice point

It is the temperature (i) of equilibrium of ice and water at standard pressure; (ii) at which pure water freezes.

Ideal solution

Also called ideal mixture, it is a solution which follows Raoult's law, in which the enthalpy of a solution is zero.

Ignition temperature

It is the minimum temperature at which combustion takes place spontaneously.

Imides

It is a group of organic compounds made of two carbonyl groups attached to nitrogen.

Imines

It is a group of compounds having a carbon-nitrogen double bond.

Implosion

In this process, objects are destructed by collapsing inwardly due to evacuation.

Indene

Derived from coal or petroleum, this colourless, inflammable, polycyclic liquid hydrocarbon is used for industrial purposes.

Indicator

It is an organic compound which changes colours in solutions of different acidities or alkanities.

Indigo

This blue-violet dye is derived from tropical plants and also created artificially.

Indium [In]

Occurring naturally in zinc, this rare, soft, silvery-white metallic element, with atomic number 49 is used in electronics and mirrors.

Indole [C_8H_7N]

Found in coal tar, it is a crystalline, organic, aromatic, heterocyclic compound and is used for industrial applications.

Inductive effect

It is an effect of the transmission of charge through the sigma bond framework by electrostatic induction.

Inert gases

Another name of noble gases, it is a non-reactive gas occupying the last column of the periodic table, and is used during chemical synthesis.

Infrared radiation [IR]

It is an invisible radiation with wavelengths longer than visible light but shorter than radio waves (frequency range between 1 and 430 THz approx.).

Infrared spectroscopy

It is an analytical method to identify functional groups and chemical functionalities of waxes and used oil.

Inhibition

It is the decelerating or barring of a process or reaction by a specific substance.

Inhibitory catalyst

It is a catalyst that slows down the reaction rate.

Inorganic chemistry

It is the branch of chemistry involving properties of inorganic compounds.

Insulator

It is a device which resists electric current and is a poor heat conductor.

Insulin

Produced in the pancreas, this naturally occurring hormone or synthetic form of this substance is used in the treatment of diabetes.

Integrated rate equation

This equation gives the concentration of a reactant in relation to time.

Interhalogens

These are formed by the reaction of halogens with each other.

Intermolecular forces

These are forces between individual particles of a substance.

Interstitial compound

This binary compound is formed when an atom of small radius occupies an interstitial space in a metal lattice of another element.

Inversion

It is a reaction leading to a shift from one optically active configuration to the opposite configuration.

Iodic acid [HIO_3]

Prepared by oxidation of iodine, this soluble, strong, crystalline acid is used to standardize solutions.

Iodine [I]

This naturally occurring non-metallic element with atomic number 53 belongs to the halogens and is used in medicines, dyes, etc.

Iodine value

Also known as iodine number, it is a measure of the number of unsaturated carbon-carbon double bonds present in the molecules of fats and oils.

Iodomethane

Also called methyl iodide, this thick, colourless, volatile liquid is used in organic synthesis, and also as a pesticide.

Ion

It is an atom or a group of atoms carrying an electric charge.

Ion exchange

It is a phenomenon in which an exchange of ions between an electrolyte solution and a complex (insoluble solid) takes place.

Ionic bond

It is a kind of chemical bond in which two particles (atom or molecule) are bonded to each other by the means of electrostatic attraction.

Ionic radius

It is the radius (distance between the centre of the nucleus and the outer edge) of an ion in an ionized state.

Ionic strength

It relates to measuring the concentration of ions and strength of an electric field in a given solution.

Ionisation

It is a process of ionizing, in which dissociation of atoms occurs due to chemical reaction or radiation.

Iridium [Ir]

This hard, brittle, dense, silvery-white metallic element with atomic number 77, belongs to the platinum group, and is used for industrial and medical purposes.

Iron [Fe]

This strong, heavy, hard, magnetic, silver-grey metallic element of atomic number 26 is widely used for commercial purposes.

Iron chloride

It refers to a chloride of iron: (i) iron dichloride; (ii) iron trichloride.

Iron oxides

These are chemical compounds made of iron and oxygen such as magnetite, etc.

Iso

This prefix refers to a compound with the same chemical formula as another but with a different structure.

Isocyanic acid [HNCO]

It is a colourless, volatile, toxic acid which consists of carbon, hydrogen, nitrogen, and oxygen, and is used in manufacturing plastics, adhesives, etc.

Isoelectric point

It is the pH at which a particular molecule is electrically neutral (no net charge).

Isoelectronic

It refers to two or more entities with the same number of electrons or similar electronic structure but consisting of different elements.

Isomerism

It is the condition of being an isomer.

Isomers

These are substances or compounds with the same molecular weight but different structural formula.

Isomorphism

It refers to the similarity in appearance (form or shape) but is genetically different.

Isoprene

Derived from petroleum, it is an unsaturated, volatile, liquid hydrocarbon which is used in the production of natural and synthetic rubbers.

Isotherm

It is a (i) curve displaying changes in volume and pressure at a constant temperature; (ii) line linking locations having the same temperature at a given point.

Isotopes

These are radioactive forms of an element that have different numbers of neutrons in the nuclei and therefore differ in relative atomic mass.

Isotropic

It refers to a physical property of a substance possessing the same value when measured in any direction.

Itaconic acid

Occurring in the fermentations of sugars, it is a white, water-soluble, non-toxic, crystalline carboxylic acid and is used in the construction industry.

IUPAC

It is known as the International Union of Pure and Applied Chemistry.

❑

Jacinth

Sometimes also called hyacinth, it is a red-orange transparent variety of zircon, which is mainly used as a semi-precious stone in jewellery.

Jade

It is a hard, green-coloured, semi-precious stone consisting of jadeite or nephrite, which is used for making jewellery.

Jahn-Teller effect

Named after Hermann Arthur Jahn and Edward Teller, it refers to the geometrical distortion of non-linear molecules under specific conditions.

Jasper

It is an opaque form of chalcedony in several colours (red, yellow, brown, dark green) which is used as gemstone in jewellery-making.

Jeweller's rouge

This mild polishing abrasive, which is red in colour (red rouge), is used in jewellery and lens-making.

j-j coupling

This mechanism is used when the spin-orbit interaction is powerful in comparison to the electrostatic interaction.

Joule

It is a unit of energy in the SI system.

Juniperic acid [$C_{16}H_{32}O_3$]

This crystalline hydroxy acid is derived from the exudations of some conifers.

❑

K capture

It is the absorption of a K shell electron by a proton resulting in the formation of a neutron.

Kalinite

This fibrous mineral is a hydrous sulphate of potassium and aluminum, and is different from isometric potassium alum.

Karbutilate [$C_{14}H_{21}N_3O_3$]

It is a cream-coloured solid, which is used as herbicides and at plant sites.

Katharometer

It is a device used for measuring thermal conductivity.

Kekule structure

It relates to the hexagonal structure of benzene and some rings of atoms that are surprisingly stable.

Keratin

It belongs to the class of insoluble fibrous proteins, which form the main component of hair, nails, horns, etc.

Ketals

These are acetals derived from a ketone, in which the molecules having a carbon bonded to two– OR groups.

Ketene

It is (i) an organic compound of the form R′R″C=C=O; (ii) an acrid, colourless reactive gas called ethenone, which is used in chemical synthesis.

Ketones

These are organic compounds in which a carbonyl group is bound to alkyl or aryl groups.

Kinetic energy

It is the mechanical energy that matter has due to its motion.

Kinetics

It is the study related to the forces that cause movement of bodies.

Kjeldahl's method

Named after Johan Kjeldahl, it is a technique applied for determining the presence of nitrogen in substances.

Knot theory

It is the theory that studies, classifies and disentangles mathematical knots.

Kojic acid

This natural product, derived from fungus, having auto oxidising properties is used mainly as a skin treatment product.

Kovar

It is an alloy of iron, nickel, and cobalt with thermal expansion properties, and is used in as an electroplated conductor in electronic parts.

Krypton [Kr]

It is a colourless, inert, gaseous element of the noble gas series with its atomic number as 36. Derived from the distillation of liquid air, it is used in photography.

Kurchatovium

Now called rutherfordium (Rf), this artificial radioactive element with atomic number 104, is the first of the transactinide elements.

❑

Lactam

Formed by heating amino acids, this cyclic amide is tautomeric to lactim.

Lactate

It is a salt or ester of lactic acid ($C_3H_6O_3$).

Lactim

It is a cyclic carboximidic acid compound, defined by an endocyclic carbon-nitrogen double bond, and is tautomeric with lactam.

Lactones

Obtained from hydroxyl acid, it is a cyclic intramolecular ester which has industrial uses.

Lactose

This sugar (disaccharide consisting of glucose and galactose) is present in milk.

Langmuir-Blodgett film

It is a set of monolayers, or layers of organic material one molecule thick, accumulated on a solid substratum.

Lanthanide contraction

It is a decrease in the ionicradii of the elements in the lanthanide series when it goes from left to right in the periodic table.

Lanthanoids

Commonly known as lanthanides, these constitute any element from atomic numbers 57 to 71.

Lanthanum [La]

This silver-white, soft, rare, metallic element with atomic number 57 is the first element in the lanthanide series and is categorized as a rare earth.

Laser

It is an acronym for a device that produces a strong beam of coherent monochromatic light by stimulated emission of radiation.

Laser spectroscopy

This type of spectroscopy is used for measuring spectral line frequencies and understanding basic atomic processes.

Latent heat

It is the heat which is released or absorbed by a substance during a change of phase without any temperature change.

Latex

Derived through polymerization, it is a water emulsion of a synthetic rubber, which is utilized in coatings, adhesives, etc.

Laughing gas

Technically called nitrous oxide, it is an odourless inhalation agent, which is mainly used as an anaesthetic.

Lauric acid

Another name for dodecanoic acid, this saturated fatty acid is a white powder with mild soap-like smell and is found in natural fats and oils.

Law of conservation of energy

This law explains that energy cannot be generated or destructed, but it can be changed from one form to another.

Law of conservation of matter

This law states that there is no noticeable change in the quantity of matter during a chemical reaction.

Law of definite proportions

This law of constant proportions states that different samples of a pure substance always contain the same elements combined in the same proportions by mass.

Law of mass action

This law explains that the rate of a reaction is proportional to the molecular concentrations of the reacting substances.

Lawrencium [Lr]

This transuranic, radioactive metallic element of the actinide series, with atomic number 103, is synthesized from californium.

Lead [Pb]

Found in many ores, this soft, dense, heavy, toxic metallic element of atomic number 82 is used in alloys, radioactive materials, paints, etc.

Lead acetate [$Pb([CH_3CO)_2$]

Prepared by treating lead oxide with acetic acid, this sweet, toxic, water-soluble, white crystalline substance is used for making enamels and dyeing cotton.

Lead carbonate [$PbCO_3$]

Industrially made from lead acetate and carbon dioxide and also naturally occurring as the mineral cerussite, this white amorphous powder is used in the manufacture of exterior paints, ceramics, etc.

Lead oxide [PbO]

This inorganic compound occurs in two forms, red (tetragonal crystal structure) known as litharge; and yellow (orthorhombic crystal structure) known as massicot, which is used in the manufacture of lead glasses, ceramic glazes, etc.

Lead sulphate [$PbSO_4$]

Also known as fast white, this toxic, white, crystalline powder occurs as the mineral anglesite, and is used in car batteries.

Leclanche cell

It is a common type of dry cell. It has been named after George Leclanche who invented and patented it. The battery constituted of ammonium chloride as conducting solution, a cathode made of carbon, manganese dioxide as a depolarizer and zinc as anode. This was later modified to make dry cells.

Lectins

These are sugar-binding proteins and should not be confused with glycoproteins (which are proteins that contain sugar chains) that are extremely specific for their sugar moieties.

Lennard-Jones potential

Also called as the L-J potential, it is a mathematically simple model that describes the interaction between a pair of neutral atoms or molecules.

Lewis acid and base

Acid as defined by Gilbert N Lewis. According to it, these are defined within the context of a particular chemical reaction, in which an acid substance is an electron lone pair acceptor and base is an electron-pair donator, forming a Lewis adduct. Since Lewis defined them, they inherit his name therefore they are referred to as Lewis acid and Lewis base.

Ligand

It is a Lewis base in a coordination compound. It is an ion or molecule (functional group) that binds to a central atom to form a coordination complex.

Lignin

It is a complex aromatic polymer, a constituent of plants, which holds cellulose fibres together.

Limestone

Found in a variety of forms (crystalline and amorphous), this hard sedimentary rock, made chiefly of calcium carbonate, is used as a building material.

Limewater [$Ca(OH)_2$]

It is an alkaline solution of calcium hydroxide in water which is hardly soluble, used in tanning, sugar-processing, etc.

Limiting reactant

It is a substance that stoichiometrically limits the amount of product(s) that can be produced.

Linear accelerator

It is an instrument used for accelerating charged particles along a straight path.

Linear molecule

It is a long chain molecule which is different from the other with many branches.

Line spectrum

It is an atomic emission or absorption spectrum.

Lipase

This water-soluble enzyme secreted by the pancreas catalyzes the breakdown of fats to fatty acids.

Lipolysis

It is the hydrolysis of lipids resulting in their breakdown to release fatty acids.

Liquid aerosol

It is the colloidal suspension of liquid in gas.

Liquid crystal

It is a substance exhibiting properties of both solid and liquid, used in cameras, mobile phones, etc.

Liquid-crystal polymer

This glass fibre belongs to a group of aromatic polyester polymers, which is unreactive, inert and fire-resistant.

Lithium [Li]

This soft, light, silvery-white, univalent metallic element of the alkali metal group with atomic number 3 occurs in several minerals.

Lithium battery

It is a rechargeable battery having lithium metal or compounds as its anode.

Lithium carbonate [Li_2CO_3]

Found in nature as zabuvelite, this white powder is a compound of lithium, carbon and oxygen used in the manufacture of glass, medicines, etc.

Lithium hydroxide [LiOH]

This colourless, corrosive, water-soluble, hygroscopic crystalline material is used for the removal of carbon dioxide from a closed atmosphere.

Lithium sulphate [Li_2SO_4]

It is a colourless to slightly yellow viscous liquid, water-soluble, inorganic lithium salt of sulphuric acid.

Litmus

Obtained from lichens, this water-soluble mixture of different dyes turns red under acid states and blue under alkaline states.

London forces

Also called dispersion forces, these are weak and short-range attractive forces between temporary dipoles with a short life.

London formula

It describes a pair of electrons residing on one atom and not shared by other atoms.

Lone pair

It is a valence electron pair that does not participate in bonding.

Low spin complex

It is a crystal field designation for an inner orbital complex.

Lowest unoccupied molecular orbital

Abbreviated as LUMO, it refers to the lowest-energy unoccupied orbital in a molecule influencing chemical properties.

Luminol test

It is a presumptive test, where this pigment is used by a number of tests used to determine the presence of blood.

Lutetium [Lu]

This rare, silver-white, trivalent metallic element of the lanthanide series, with atomic number 71, is used in refineries, manufacture of light bulbs, etc.

Lux [lx]

It is the SI unit of illuminance and luminous emittance.

Lyate ion

This anion is obtained by the deprotonation of a solvent molecule.

Lye

Commonly known as caustic soda, it is a strong, corrosive, alkaline solution of sodium or potassium hydroxide, which is used for many household purposes.

Lyophilic

It relates to the tendency of a colloid which has an affinity for the dispersion medium and is not easily precipitated. They are soluble in water, no additional stabilizers are required, stable and easy to prepare.

Lyophobic

It describes colloids which have no affinity for the dispersion medium and are easily precipitated. They are not soluble in water, need additional stabilizers, unstable and rather difficult to prepare.

❑

Macromolecule

Usually formed by polymerisation, this complex molecule which has a very large number of atoms is found in plants and animals.

Macroscopic

It is something which is sufficiently not large to be visible to the naked eye.

Magic acid [FSO_3H-SbF_5]

This super acid, a mixture of fluorosulphonic acid and antimony pentafluoride, is used to catalyze isomerisation of saturated hydrocarbons.

Magnadur

This ceramic material consisting of sintered iron oxide and barium is used for manufacturing permanent magnets.

Magnalium

This common alloy is mainly a mixture of aluminum and magnesium finds its use in engineering, manufacturing fireworks, etc.

Magnesia

Another name for magnesium oxide (MgO), this naturally occurring, colourless, hygroscopic, solid mineral is magnesium's source, and is used in cement, medicines, etc.

Magnesium [Mg]

This silver-white, light, ductile, bivalent metallic element of the alkaline earth series of atomic number 12 is used for manufacturing alloys, flash bulbs, etc.

Magnesium carbonate [$MgCO_3$]

Naturally occurring as magnesite or dolomite, this white, crystalline solid is used as an absorbent, colouring agent, etc.

Magnesium chloride [$MgCl_2$]

Obtained from magnesium carbonate and hydrogen chloride, this water-soluble compound is an ionic halide used in food items, medicines, etc.

Magnesium hydroxide [$Mg(OH)_2$]

This milk-like white, crystalline powder is used mainly in medicines.

Magnesium sulphate [$MgSO_4$]

This white, water-soluble chemical compound which contains magnesium, sulphur and oxygen is used in the agriculture and pharmaceutical industry.

Magnetism

Generated by the movement of electric charge, this physical phenomenon leads to attractive and repulsive forces between objects.

Magnetite [Fe_3O_4]

A form of iron ore and iron oxide, this grey-black, ferrimagnetic mineral is a member of the spinel group, and is used for many industrial purposes.

Magnetochemistry

It is a chemistry that analyses the effect of a magnetic field on molecular structure.

Maleic acid

It is an organic compound found in unripe fruit. Prepared by distilling malic acid, this colourless, dicarboxylic, crystalline acid is used chiefly to make polyester resins and as an oil and fat preservative.

Maleic anhydride [$C_2H_2(CO)_2O$]

It is a caustic, crystalline, cyclic acid anhydride of maleic acid and has an acrid odour, used mainly for manufacturing resins.

Malonic acid [$CH_2(COOH)_2$]

Derived from the oxidation of malic acid, this colourless, crystalline, dicarboxylic acid is used for the manufacture of barbiturates.

Maltose

This white crystalline sugar (disaccharide) is formed by the breakdown of starch.

Manganate

This negatively charged molecular entity is the salt of manganic acid in which the anion consists of manganese and oxygen, and is used in organic synthesis.

Manganese [Mn]

Found naturally in many minerals, this hard, brittle, grey, non-magnetic, polyvalent metallic element of the transition series, having atomic number 25, is used in the manufacture of steel, aluminum alloys, etc.

Manganic compounds

These are compounds of manganese in its +3 oxidation state.

Mannich reaction

It is an electrophilic substitution reaction, which is used for the organic synthesis of natural and medicinal compounds.

Mannitol [$C_6H_8(OH)_6$]

Found in many plants, it is a white, sweet, crystalline compound that is used in food items, medicines, etc.

Mannose

Found in certain plants, it is a sugar monomer of the aldohexose series of carbohydrates.

Manometer

It is a two-armed barometer (pressure gauge) for comparing pressures of a gas.

Marble

This hard, crystalline, metamorphic stone with streaks that requires polishing is used for sculpture and architecture.

Marsh gas

When vegetation decomposes in water, it emits methane gas.

Marsh's test

It is an extremely sensitive test to detect minimal amounts of arsenic.

Maser

An acronym for microwave amplification by stimulated emission of radiation; it is an amplifier which emits coherent microwave radiation like laser.

Mass

Generally measured in grams and kilograms, it is a measure of the amount of matter in an object.

Mass action

It is the conception which a large number of atoms reacting randomly by themselves can form a larger pattern.

Mass spectrometer

It is a device for measuring the charge-to-mass ratio of charged particles.

Mass spectroscopy

This spectroscopy is an analytical method to measure the masses of small electrically charged particles.

Matrix

It is the main constituent of a composite material.

Mechanism

Through these sequential steps, the reactants are transformed into substances.

Meitnerium [Mt]

Produced by atomic collisions, this unstable, radioactive, transuranic element of atomic number 109 is used in nuclear fissions.

Melamine

Prepared by heating cyanamide, this colourless, crystalline compound is used chiefly for manufacturing plastics and resins.

Mellitic acid [$C_6(COOH)_6$]

Also called graphitic acid, this crystalline acid is prepared synthetically and naturally occurs as the mineral mellite.

Melting point

Also called the freezing point, it is the temperature at which liquid and solid are in equilibrium.

Menthol [$C_{10}H_{20}O$]

Prepared synthetically or derived from peppermint, this crystalline, waxy, white substance with a minty taste, is used in food, medicines, etc.

Mercaptans

Synonymous with thiols, it is a group of sulphur compounds, which has disagreeable sulphur-like smell added to natural gas for detection of gas leaks.

Mercury [Hg]

This heavy, silvery-white, toxic, univalent, metallic element of atomic number 80 which is liquid at room temperature, is used mainly in thermometers.

Mercury cell

Also called mercury battery, this primary cell is an electrochemical battery that cannot be recharged.

Mercury fulminate [$Hg(CNO)_2$]

This primary explosive is extremely sensitive to friction and shock, is chiefly used in detonators, percussion caps, etc.

Mercury oxide [HgO]

Another name for mercuric oxide, this red or orange-coloured, toxic substance is solid at room temperature, and is used for the production of mercury, batteries, etc.

Mescaline

Found in Mexican cactus, it is a hallucinogenic and intoxicating compound, which is used primarily as an entheogen.

Meta

It is a prefix referring to the placement of two substituents on a benzene ring divided by one carbon.

Metabolism

It refers to the chemical reactions that takes place in living organisms to grow and reproduce to maintain life.

Metal

It is a solid substance which is usually hard, shiny, and ductile with good electrical and thermal conductivity. Most of the elements are metals like iron, copper, etc.

Metaldehyde [$CH_3CHO)_4$]

This cyclic tetramer of acetaldehyde is an organic compound used as a pesticide.

Metallic bond

It is a kind of bonding in which electronic conduction takes place and the valence electrons freely migrate from one atom to another.

Metallocene

This compound is made of two cyclopentadienyl anions bound to a metal centre in the oxidation state II, with the resultant formula $(C_5H_5)_2M$.

Metalloid

These are elements with the properties of both metals and non-metals.

Metallurgy

It describes the complete processes of extracting metals from ores.

Metastable state

It is an excited stationary energy state of an atom with an unusually long lifetime.

Metathesis

These are reactions in which two compounds react, producing two new compounds, without any changes in the oxidation number.

Methacrylic acid [$C_4H_6O_2$]

This unsaturated, carboxylic acid is a colourless, syrupy, foul-smelling, water-soluble liquid, which is used to manufacture synthetic resins and plastics.

Methane [CH_4]

This flammable gas lacking colour and odour is the simplest member of the alkane series of hydrocarbons used mainly as a fuel.

Methanol [CH_3OH]

Prepared mainly by oxidizing methane, this simplest aliphatic alcohol, also called methyl alcohol, is a light, toxic, colourless, volatile, inflammable liquid, which is used as a solvent, fuel, anti-freeze, etc.

Methylamine [CH_3NH_2]

Derived from ammonia, this toxic, colourless gas is the simplest aliphatic amine which is used for several industrial purposes.

Methylation

It refers to adding of a methyl group to a substrate or the substitution of an atom or group by a methyl group.

Methylbenzene

Derived from petroleum or coal tar, this colourless, water-insoluble, inflammable liquid, also called toluene, is used as a solvent for gums and lacquers and in high-octane fuels.

Methyl bromide [CH_3Br]

Also known as bromomethane, this poisonous, colourless, odourless gas obtained naturally and industrially is used mainly as a pesticide.

Methyl chloride [CH_3Cl]

Synonymous with chloromethane, this colourless liquid with a faint, sweet smell belongs to the haloalkanes group, and is used in production of many chemicals.

Methylene

It refers to themethylene group (chemical species) in which the bivalent radical CH_2 is derived from methane with the loss of two hydrogen atoms.

Methyl ethanoate [CH_3COOCH_3]

Also called methyl acetate, this carboxylate ester is a pleasant-smelling, inflammable liquid is used in the manufacture of glues, paints, etc.

Methyl group

This univalent radical group is a hydrophobic alkyl functional group with the formula, $-CH_3$, which is derived from methane.

Methyl methacrylate [$CH_2=C(CH_3)COOCH_3$]

A methyl ester of methacrylic acid, this colourless, volatile liquid is used to manufacture polymethyl methacrylate.

Methyl red

This dark, red crystalline powder is an indicator dye that turns red in acidic solutions.

Methyl violet

A purple-coloured dye which is used in textiles, paints, etc.

Mica

Found naturally as minute scales in rocks, this shiny, silicate mineral with a layered structure is used as an insulator, effect pigment, etc.

Micelle

Found in certain colloidal electrolytic solutions, it is an electrically charged particle made from polymeric molecules.

Micro

It is a prefix meaning one millionth.

Microscopic

It is something which is so minute that it cannot be seen with a naked eye, and becomes visible only with the help of a microscope.

Microwaves

These electromagnetic waves have wavelengths shorter than a radio wave but longer than an infrared wave.

Microwave spectroscopy

This is used to analyse molecular resonances in the microwave spectrum.

Migration

It explains the non-random motion within a molecule itself of an atom from one position to another.

Millon's reagent

This solution of mercury in nitric acid is used to determine the presence of soluble proteins.

Mineral acid

Another name for inorganic acid, it is obtained from one or more inorganic compounds, and forms hydrogen ions.

Moiety

These are particular functional groups of atoms within molecules responsible for the chemical reactions that take place.

Molality

It is the concentration expressed as number of moles of solute per kilogram of solvent.

Molar

It is assigning a solution consisting of one mole of solute per litre of solution.

Molar conductivity

It describes the conductivity of an electrolyte solution divided by the molar concentration of the electrolyte thus measuring the efficiency of an electrolyte to conduct electricity.

Molar heat capacity

It is the amount of heat energy required to raise the temperature of one mole of a substance.

Molarity

It is the number of moles of solute per litre of solution.

Molar volume

Also called molecular volume, it is the volume occupied by one mole of a substance at a given temperature and pressure.

Mole

It is the SI unit of amount of substance.

Molecular equation

It refers to an equation for a chemical reaction.

Molecular formula

It refers to a formula that shows the actual number of atoms present in a molecule of a substance.

Molecular orbital theory

This theory is based upon the postulated existence of molecular orbitals.

Molecular weight

It is the mass of one molecule of a non-ionic substance in atomic mass units.

Molecularity

It refers to the number of particles which are involved as reactants in an elementary reaction.

Molecular modelling

It covers all theoretical and computational methods used to model the behaviour of molecules.

Molecular recognition

It refers to the particular processes between two or more molecules through non-covalent bonding, thus producing a larger structure.

Molecular sieve

It is a crystalline material containing pores of a precise and uniform size, allowing the passage of molecules below a certain size.

Molecule

It is the smallest particle of a substance which can exist independently.

Mole fraction

It is the number of moles of a component of a mixture divided by the total number of moles in the mixture.

Molybdenum [Mo]

This brittle, silver-grey polyvalent metallic element of the transition series of atomic number 42 is used for hardening alloy steels.

Monatomic molecule

It is a kind of molecule which has only one atom.

Monobasic acid

This acid contains only one hydrogen ion to donate to a base in a chemical reaction.

Monomer

It is an atom or molecule that can be bonded chemically to other similar molecules to form a polymer.

Monovalent

It means having a valence of one.

Mordant

It is a substance, usually an inorganic oxide, that combines with a dye or stain, thereby setting it on a material.

Morse potential

Named after Philip M. Morse, it is an empirical potential that explains the stretching of a chemical bond.

Mosaic gold

Technically called stannic sulphide, it is a yellow crystalline powder (pigment), which is used mainly in gilding wood and metal work.

Mother nuclide

It is a nuclide that undergoes nuclear decay.

Multiple bond

It is the double bond between the two carbon atoms that has more than one pair of electrons.

Multiplet

It is a class of closely associated things such as atomic energy levels.

Muscovite

Naturally found in rocks, this colourless or brown, or grey-coloured form of mica with potassium, also called common mica, is used as an insulator.

Mustard gas

It is a colourless, posionous war gas containing sulphide based compounds.

Mutarotation

It is the change in optical rotation of a sugar seen right after it dissolves in a liquid solution.

Myristic acid [$CH_3(CH_2)_{12}COOH$]

Found naturally in animal and vegetable fats, this saturated fatty acid, also called tetradecanoic acid, is used in medicines and cosmetics.

❑

Nano

It is a prefix which means one-billionth.

Nanotechnology

This type of technology relates to the dimensions of things which are less than a hundred nanometers.

Napalm

Made of gasoline thickened with soaps, this inflammable, thick substance is mainly used in military operations (bombs, flamethrowers).

Naphthalene

Prepared by the distillation of coal tar, this white, crystalline compound with a strong odour, also called napthalin, is used chiefly as a fumigant in moth balls.

Naphthols

These two phenols are derivates of naphthalene.

Naphthyl group

This group ($C_{10}H_7$–) is derived after the removal of a hydrogen atom from naphthalene.

Native state

This state is when an element occurs in a free state in nature.

Natural gas

Found naturally as a fossil fuel, this highly inflammable gas is made mainly of methane and other hydrocarbons, and is used as a fuel.

Natural radioactivity

It is the spontaneous decomposition of an atom.

Nematic crystal

It is a kind of translucent liquid crystal in which the waves pass through the liquid and lead the polarization of light waves to change.

Neodymium [Nd]

Found naturally in monazite and bastnasite, this silvery-white, trivalent, metallic element of the lanthanide series with atomic number 60, is used in the manufacture of ceramics and some alloys.

Neon [Ne]

Derived by the distillation of liquid air, it is an inert, colourless, odourless, gaseous element of the noble gas group with atomic number 10.

Neoprene

Prepared by the polymerization of chloroprene, this synthetic, heat-resistant, rubber-like polymer, also called polychloroprene, is used in waterproofing, etc.

Neptunium

Obtained artificially and naturally, it is a radioactive, transuranic metallic element of the actinide series having atomic number 93.

Nernst equation

It is used for calculating the equilibrium potentials for non-standard conditions.

Nerve agents

Another name for nerve gases, these toxic gases is a class of organophosphates which has harmful effects on the nervous system.

Nessler's reagent

This alkaline solution of potassium mercuric iodide is used as a test for the presence of ammonia.

Net ionic equation

It is a consequence of cancelling spectator ions and removing brackets from a total ionic equation.

Neutral

It is something which is neither acid nor alkaline.

Neutralisation

It is the reaction of an acid with a base to form a salt and water.

Neutron

It is a neutral subatomic particle with a mass of 1.0087 amu.

Neutron diffraction

It is a technique by which neutrons are used to ascertain the atomic and magnetic structure of a substance.

Newman projection

It is prepared by visualizing along a carbon-carbon single (double) bond.

Nickel [Ni]

This hard, ductile, corrosion-resistant, silvery-white, ferromagnetic metallic element of atomic number 28 is used as an alloying agent, catalyst, etc.

Nickel carbonyl[Ni(CO)$_4$]

This organonickel compound is a pale-yellow, volatile, poisonous, metal carbonyl is used for coating metals and manufacturing pure nickel.

Nickelous compounds

These are compounds of nickel in its +2 oxidation state.

Nickel oxide [NiO]

This compound is the only well-known oxide of nickel with two forms (Ni_2O_3 and NiO_2) is used in fuel cells and batteries.

Nicotine [$C_{10}H_{14}N_2$]

This toxic, colourless, oily liquid is the main component of tobacco which is used in insecticides.

Nictonic acid

Another name for niacin, it is derived from pyridine and is important to maintain life.

Ninhydrin

This synthetic crystalline substance is used to detect primary and secondary amines.

Niobium [Nb]

Found in niobite, this ductile, soft, silver-grey metallic element of the transition series of atomic number 41 is used in steel production and superconducting alloys.

Nitrate

It is a salt or ester of nitric acid, with the group $-NO_3$.

Nitration

It is a chemical reaction in which a nitro group is introduced into a chemical compound.

Nitrene

It is the nitrogen analogue of a carbene. It is a reactive intermediate involved in many chemical reactions.

Nitric acid [HNO_3]

Prepared by distilling nitrates with sulphuric acid, this colourless or yellow, toxic, corrosive, strong acid is used in the production of fertilizers, rocket fuels, etc.

Nitrides

These binary compounds contain nitrogen and a more electropositive element. They are a large class with a wide range of properties and applications. They are used in refactories.

Nitrile

It is a group of organic compounds with the cyano radical -CN.

Nitrite

It is a salt or ester of nitrous acid, having the anion NO_2^-.

Nitroalkane

It is a group of compounds containing the monovalent nitro radical $-NO_2$.

Nitrobenzene [$C_6H_5NO_2$]

Prepared by nitrating benzene, it is an oily, poisonous, water-soluble, pale-yellow, liquid with an almond-like smell and is used in chemical synthesis.

Nitrocellulose

Obtained by treating cellulose with concentrated nitric acid, this inflammable, cotton-like substance, is used in explosives and collodion, etc.

Nitro compounds

These explosive, impure compounds have one or more nitro functional groups.

Nitrogen

It is an inert, colourless, odourless, non-reactive gaseous element with atomic number 7, and is used as a propellant, coolant, etc.

Nitrogen cycle

It is a complex series of chemical processes by which nitrogen is continually recycled in the environment.

Nitrogen dioxide [NO_2]

Formed by the oxidation of nitric oxide, this brown-coloured, toxic gas is used as an intermediate in the manufacture of nitric acid.

Nitrogen monoxide [NO]

Commonly known as nitric oxide, this poisonous gas consisting of nitrogen and oxygen is chiefly used as an intermediate in the chemical industry.

Nitrogen mustards

These toxic, cytotoxic alkylating agents structurally similar to mustard gas are utilized for the treatment of cancer.

Nitrogenases

Found in plants, this group of enzymes catalyses reactions which results in the conversion of N2 molecules in the air to ammonia.

Nitroglycerine

Derived by nitrating glycerol, this thick, yellow, toxic, greasy, highly flammable liquid is used in explosives and medicines.

Nitrosonium ion

It is an ion (NO^+) created from nitrous acid in which the nitrogen atom is bonded to an oxygen atom with a bond order of 3.

Nitrous acid [HNO_2]

Prepared by the action of acids on nitrites, this unstable and weak acid is known only in solution and as nitrite salts.

Nitryl ion

Made by the protonation of nitric acid, this ion (NO_2^+), commonly called nitronium ion, is a reactive cation.

Nobelium

Obtained by bombarding curium with carbon ions, it is a radioactive, transuranic, synthetic metallic element of the actinide series with atomic number 102.

Noble gases

Another name for rare gases, these are elements of the periodic Group 0.

Nonahydrate

It is a hydrate containing nine molecules of water of crystallization per molecule.

Nonanoic acid [$C_9H_{18}O_2$]

Also called pelargonic acid, this clear, oily liquid with a disagreeable smell forms esters and is used in cosmetics and as flavourings.

Non-electrolyte

It is a substance whose aqueous solutions does not conduct electricity.

Non-metal

It is an element which lacks the chemical or physical properties of a metal.

Non-polar bond

It is a covalent bond in which electron density is symmetrically distributed.

Non-polar compound

This compound is equal and neutral, without a net charge.

Nuclear fission

It is a nuclear reaction in which a heavy nucleus splits into nuclei of intermediate masses simultaneously releasing energy.

Nuclear magnetic resonance

Abbreviated as NMR, it is a property relating to the resonance of protons to radiation in a magnetic field.

Nuclear reaction

It is a process which changes the composition, structure of a nucleus and evolves or absorbs large amount of energy.

Nucleons

These are the particles comprising the nucleus (proton or neutron).

Nucleophile

This species, a nucleus-lover, is a reagent which donates a pair of electrons in the reaction in question.

Nucleophilic substitution

In this kind of substitution reaction, an electron-rich nucleophile reacts with a compound substituting another nucleophile.

Nucleosynthesis

It is the phenomenon of forming new atomic nuclei from pre-existing nucleons.

Nucleus

It is a minute, dense, positively charged centre of an atom comprising protons, neutrons and other particles.

Nuclide

It describes an atomic species in contrast to isotopes, which refer only to different atomic forms of a single element.

Nylon

Belonging to family of strong synthetic fibres, this resilient, lightweight, elastic polymer is used in the manufacture of sheets, molded objects, etc.

❑

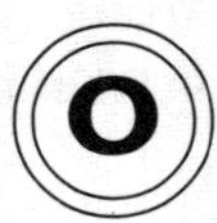

Ochre

It is a non-toxic, yellowish-orange, earth pigment consisting of silica, aluminum and ferric oxide, which is used as a painting pigment and in medicines.

Octadecenoic acid

It is a class of unsaturated fatty acids found in many animal and vegetable sources.

Octahedral

It refers to the molecules and polyatomic ions that have one atom in the centre and six atoms at the corners of an octahedron.

Octahydrate

It is a hydrate consisting of eight molecules of water of crystallization per molecule.

Octane [$CH_3(CH_2)_6CH_3$]

Derived from petroleum refining, this isomeric, saturated, colourless, flammable hydrocarbon of the alkane series, it is used as a fuel and solvent.

Octane number

It is a number which points to the antiknock properties of a fuel.

Octavalent

It is something which has a valence of eight.

Octet

It is a stable group of eight electrons with a single shell in an atom.

Oil

Extracted from animals and plants, this heavy, viscous, flammable, water-insoluble liquid is a triester of glycerol and unsaturated fatty acids.

Oleate

It is a salt or ester of oleic acid.

Oleic acid

Found in many fats and oils, it is a monosaturated, colourless fatty acid used in cosmetics, lubricating oils, etc.

Oleum

Also called fuming sulphuric acid, it is a thick, corrosive liquid containing concentrated sulphuric acid with sulphur trioxide in solution.

Oligopeptide

It is a peptide whose molecules have a small number of amino acids.

Oligosaccharide

It is a carbohydrate whose molecules are made of a small number of component sugars (monosaccharides).

Onium ion

This ion is formed by adding a proton to a neutral molecule.

Opal

It is a semitransparent mineral comprising hydrated silica of different colours, mainly used as a gemstone.

Open sextet

It is a species that has only six electrons in the highest energy level of the central element.

Optical activity

It is the rotation of plane polarized light by one of a pair of optical isomers.

Optical glass

It is a clear, homogeneous, pure glass of known refractive index used for lenses.

Optical isomers

Another name for enantiomers, these are stereoisomers that differ only by being non-superimposable mirror images of each other.

Orbital

It is the pattern of electron density that may be formed in a molecule.

Order

It is the order of reaction described as the power to which its concentration term in the rate equation is raised.

Ore

It is a natural deposit from which a metal or mineral can be extracted.

Oregonator

It is a theoretical model of the chemical dynamics of the oscillatory Belousov-Zhabotinsky reaction.

Organic chemistry

It is the chemistry of substances which contain carbon.

Organometallic compound

It is a compound with an alkyl or aryl radical bonded to a metal.

Organophosphorous compound

It is a degradable organic compound comprising carbon-phosphorus bonds.

Orpiment [As_2S_3]

Occurring in conjunction with realgar, it is a bright-yellow, monoclinic mineral containing arsenic trisulphide.

Ortho

It is a prefix denoting substitution at two adjacent carbon atoms in a benzene ring.

Oscillating reaction

It is a kind of chemical reaction of compounds in which the concentration of one or more components displays periodic alterations.

Osmiridium

A natural alloy of osmium and iridium, this rare, hard, corrosion-resistant mineral is used in needles, pen nibs, munitions, etc.

Osmium [Os]

This dense, heavy, hard, silver metallic element of the transition series having atomic number 76 is used in making alloys.

Osmometer

It is a device for measuring osmotic pressure or strength of a solution.

Osmosis

It is the process in which molecules of a solvent move through a semipermeable membrane from a dilute solution into a more concentrated solution.

Osmotic pressure

It is the hydrostatic pressure generated on the surface of a semipermeable membrane as a result of osmosis.

Ostwald ripening

It is a phenomenon occurring in solutions (solid or liquid), explaining the alteration of an inhomogeneous structure over time.

Ostwald's dilution law

This law states a relationship between the dissociation constant and the degree of dissociation of a weak electrolyte.

Outer orbital complex

It is valence bond designation for a complex in which the metal ion uses d-orbitals in the outermost shell in hybridization.

Overlap

It is the interaction of orbitals on different atoms in the same space.

Overpotential

It refers to the difference between a half-reaction's thermodynamic and observed potentials.

Oxalate

It is a salt or ester of oxalic acid.

Oxalic acid [$C_2H_2O_4$]

Found in plants, it is a colourless, sour-tasting toxic, crystalline acid, and it is used for bleaching, cleansing, removing rust, etc.

Oxazole

This volatile, aromatic liquid is a weak base whose molecule contains a five-membered ring, and is used in medicines.

Oxidant

Another name for oxidising agent, it is a substance which oxidises another substance.

Oxidation

It is a process of oxidising in which oxygen is added to a compound with a loss of electrons.

Oxidation number

It is an arbitrary number, which is usually used in writing formulas and balancing equations.

Oxidation-reduction

Synonymous with redox reaction, it is a chemical reaction in which oxidation and reduction takes place.

Oxides

These are binary compounds of oxygen with another element.

Oxygen [O]

It is a colourless, odourless, bivalent, most abundant gaseous element in the earth's crust with atomic number 8.

Ozonation

In this process, the ozone gas is formed in the earth's atmosphere.

Ozone [O_3]

Formed from oxygen, this colourless, poisonous gas is a strong oxidising agent, and acts as a screen for ultraviolet radiation.

Ozonides

These are a group of unstable compounds as a result of ozone being added to a double bond in an unsaturated compound.

Ozonolysis

It is a process in which alkenes react with ozone producing an ozonide.

❑

Pairing

It is an interaction of two electrons with opposite spins.

Palladium [Pd]

Naturally occurring in copper and nickel ores, this rare, silver-white, lustrous, metallic element of the platinum group with atomic number 46 resembles platinum, and is mainly used in making jewellery.

Palmitate [$C_{16}H_{32}O_2$]

This salt or ester of palmitic acid is used in cosmetics, soaps, etc.

Palmitic acid [$CH_3(CH_2)_{14}COOH$]

Derived from vegetable and animal sources, this solid saturated fatty acid is a main constituent of the oil from palm trees.

Pantothenic acid [$C_9H_{17}NO_5$]

Another name for pantothenate, it is a water-soluble vitamin of the B complex found in foods, and plays a vital rolein the oxidation of fats and carbohydrates.

Paper chromatography

It is a method for classifying and identifying mixtures that are coloured with the use of selective adsorption on a strip of paper.

Para

It is a prefix indicating substitution at diametrically opposite carbon atoms in a benzene ring.

Paraformaldehyde

This colourless, crystalline solid, the smallest polyoxymethylene, is the condensation reaction product of formaldehyde.

Paraldehyde

Prepared by treating acetaldehyde with acid, this cyclic trimer of acetaldehyde is a colourless, alcohol-soluble liquid used in medicines as a sedative, solvent, etc.

Paramagnetism

It refers to the attraction toward a magnetic field, weaker than ferromagnetism and stronger than diamagnetism.

Paraquat

This toxic, yellow, fast-acting, non-selective solid is used widely as herbicides.

Partial pressure

It is the pressure exerted by one gas in a mixture of gases.

Particulate matter

It is the fine divided solid particles suspended in polluted air.

Partition coefficient

It is the ratio of the concentrations of a solute in two immiscible substances at equilibrium.

Paschen-Back effect

It is a splitting of spectral lines seen when the source of a radiation is in the presence of a strong magnetic field.

Paschen series

It is a series of lines in the infrared spectrum of atomic hydrogen.

P-block elements

In the periodic table, it comprises the last six groups, consisting all of the non-metals, semi-metals and post-transition metals.

Peacock ore

Occurring in copper deposits, it is a sulphide mineral, also known as bornite (Cu_5FeS_4) that crystallizes in the orthorhombic system.

Percentage ionisation

It is the percentage of the weak electrolyte which ionizes in a solution of given concentration.

Penicillin

Made naturally from Penicillium fungi by certain blue molds, and synthetically as well, it is a group of antibiotics used for curing many infections and diseases.

Pentahydrate

It is a hydrate consisting of five molecules of water of crystallization per molecule.

Pentane [C_5H_{12}]

Found in petroleum-based solvents, it is a volatile liquid hydrocarbon of the alkane series with five carbon atoms, and may refer to any of three structural isomers.

Pentanedioic acid

Also called glutaric acid ($C_3H_6(COOH)_2$), it is a dicarboxylic acid with five carbon atoms, which is found in plant and animal tissues.

Pentanoic acid

Another name for valeric acid ($C_5H_{10}O_2$), it is a clear liquid carboxylic acid with an irritating smell, which isused in perfumes, flavourings, pharmaceuticals, etc.

Pentavalent

It is something which has a valence of five.

Pentose [$C_5H_{10}O_5$]

A pentose is a monosaccharide with five carbon atoms such as ribose and xylose.

Pentyl group [C_5H_{11}]

It is the univalent, isomeric groups ($CH_3CH_2CH_2CH_2CH_2$-) obtained from pentane.

Pepsin

Generated by the cells in the stomach, it is the main digestive enzyme, which breaks down proteins into peptides.

Peptide

Derived by partial hydrolysis of protein, it is an amide combining the amino group of one amino acid with the carboxyl group of another.

Perchlorate

It is a salt of perchloric acid.

Perchloric acid [$HClO_4$]

This fuming, strong, colourless, poisonous liquid with powerful oxidising properties is used as rocket fuel, and in electropolishing/etching of metals.

Pericyclic reaction

Generally, a rearrangement reaction, it is a kind of reaction in which the transition state of the molecule has a cyclic geometry, and the reaction proceeds in a concerted manner.

Periodic law

This law states that the properties of the elements are periodic functions of their atomic numbers.

Periodic table

It is an arrangement of elements according to the increasing atomic numbers based on the periodic law.

Permanent gas

It is a gas at a pressure and temperature which is incapable of liquefaction.

Permanent hardness

It is hardness of water due to the presence of the chlorides and sulphates of calcium and magnesium that cannot be removed by boiling.

Permanganate

This dark-purple salt of permanganic acid having the anion MnO_4^- with strong oxidising properties is used chiefly as a disinfectant.

Peroxides

It is a compound consisting of the peroxide anion (O_2^{2-}).

Petrochemicals

These are substances derived by the refining and processing of petroleum or natural gas.

Petroleum

Found and extracted from rock strata beneath the earth's surface, this poisonous, flammable liquid mixture of hydrocarbons of various molecular weights is refined for the production of other fuels.

Pfund series

It is the series denoting the emission spectrum of hydrogen when the electron is jumping to the fifth orbital.

Phase

It is a distinct state (solid, liquid, or gaseous) of matter in a chemical system.

Phase diagram

It displays the equilibrium temperature-pressure relationships for different phases of a substance.

Phase rule

It states the maximum numbers of phases, constituents, and degrees of freedom possible in a system.

Phenol-formaldehyde resin

Derived from the reaction of phenols with formaldehyde, it is an irregular, transparent, synthetic thermosetting resin, which is used for making circuit boards.

Phenolphthalein [$C_{20}H_{14}O_4$]

This crystalline solid, which becomes pink in alkaline solution and colourless in acidic solutions, is used as an acid–base indicator and laxative.

Phenols

Derived from coal tar, this carbolic acid is a slightly acidic, poisonous, colourless crystalline solid used as a disinfectant and in chemical manufacture as well.

Phenoxy resins

Obtained from polyhydroxy ether, it is a high-molecular-weight thermoplastic polyether resin used for coatings, adhesives, etc.

Phenylenediamine [$C_6H_4(NH_2)_2$]

Obtained from aniline, this colourless solid is used in polymers, hair dyes, etc.

Phenyl group [C_6H_5]

Also called phenyl ring, this cyclic group of atoms is related to benzene.

Phenylhydrazine [$C_6H_5NHNH_2$]

Made by oxidising aniline with sodium nitrite, this compound is used in medicines, dyes, etc.

Phonochemistry

It is the branch of chemistry related to the effects of sound and ultrasonic waves on chemical reactions.

Phosgene [$COCl_2$]

Prepared by the reaction of chlorine and carbon monoxide, it is a colourless, toxic gas known for its use in chemical warfare, and also as an industrial reagent.

Phosphates

These are salts of phosphoric acid used industrially as a coating agent.

Phosphide

It is a binary compound of phosphorus with a less electronegative element.

Phosphine [PH_3]

This compound of phosphorus and hydrogen is a colourless, flammable, poisonous gas with an unpleasant smell chiefly used as a pesticide.

Phosphinic acid

It is a class of monobasic organic acids, which can be derived by oxidation from disubstituted phosphines.

Phosphite

It is a salt of phosphorous acid.

Phosphonic acid

Also called phosphonate, it is a crystalline substance derived by reacting phosphorus trioxide and water.

Phosphorous acid [H_3PO_4]

Derived by treating phosphates with sulphuric acid, this colourless, crystalline acid, also called orthophosphoric acid, is used in fertilizers, soaps, etc.

Phosphorous [P]

Found in inorganic phosphate rocks, this poisonous, combustible, highly reactive, multivalent non-metallic element of the nitrogen family with atomic number 15 exists in two common allotropic forms: white and red phosphorous.

Photochemical oxidants

These are oxidising agents, which are created photochemically and are harmful to plants and animals.

Photochemical reaction

This reaction takes place by the action or absorption of light.

Photochemistry

It is a branch of chemistry concerned with the action or effect of light on chemical systems.

Photochromism

It is the reversible transformation of a material between two forms when exposed to electromagnetic radiation.

Photoionisation

This process is generated in a medium by the action of electromagnetic radiation, where an incident photon releases one or more electrons from a molecule.

Photolysis

It is a chemical reaction in which there is decomposition of molecules by the action or effect of light.

Photon

Also called quantum of light, it is a packet of light or electromagnetic radiation.

Photosynthesis

This process generally occurring in plants involves synthesis of compounds with the help of light, in which oxygen is generated as a byproduct.

pH scale

It is a way of measuring acidity and alkalinity of a substance, where = 7 is neutral; <7 is more basic; and >7 is more acidic.

Phthalic acid [$C_6H_4(CO_2H)_2$]

Obtained from benzene, this crystalline, colourless, aromatic, dicarboxylic acid is used in the manufacture of dyes, perfumes, etc.

Phthalocyanine

This greenish-blue crystalline dye (macrocyclic compound) of the porphyrin group forms coordination complexes with most elements of the periodic table.

Physical chemistry

The branch of chemistry concerned with the physical properties of chemical substances.

Phytostigmine

Also called serine, this a reversible cholinesterase inhibitor, which is naturally found in the Calabar bean, and is used for treating many diseases.

Pi bond

It is a kind of covalent bond in which the electron density is concentrated above and below the two atoms.

Picric acid [$C_6H_3N_3O_7$]

Derived by nitrating phenol, this bitter, yellow, toxic, strong, explosive, crystalline acid is used as a dye and in the making explosives.

Pi electron

It is an electron involved in a pi bond.

Piperidine [$(CH_2)_5NH$]

Made by the reduction of pyridine, this peppery-smelling, colourless, fuming liquid is used in the synthesis of organic compounds.

pK value

It is a value of the strength of an acid on a logarithmic scale.

Plaster of Paris

Also referred to as gypsum plaster, this white powder, a hemihydrate of calcium sulphate, is used in making casts, molds, etc.

Plastics

Made from organic polymers, these are synthetic or semisynthetic materials that can be molded into different shapes, and are used in coatings, adhesives, etc.

Platinum [Pt]

Occurring in nickel and copper ores, this heavy, precious, silvery-white metallic element with atomic number 78 is used in jewellery, electrical contacts, etc.

Platinum metals

Naturally occurring, these six metals (platinum, palladium, ruthenium, osmium, rhodium, and iridium) in the periodic table have similar properties.

Plumbate

It is a salt formed when lead dioxide reacts with basic oxides.

Plutonium [Pu]

Naturally occurring in small quantities in uranium ores and mostly manufactured in nuclear reactors, this solid, dense, silvery radioactive metallic element of the actinide series of atomic number 94, is used as a fuel, in making explosives, etc.

Pnicogens

These elements with some similar properties and some differences in oxidation states consist of nitrogen, phosphorus, arsenic, antimony, and bismuth.

Pnictides

It is a binary compound of a pnicogen and an electropositive element.

Poison

It is a chemical substance that (i) inhibits another substance or a reaction; (ii) can be harmful and even fatal if consumed by chemical means.

Polar bond

It is a covalent bond in which the distribution of electron density is not symmetrical.

Polar compound

It is a chemical compound whose molecules have polar covalent bonds and display electrically positive characteristics at one extreme and negative at the other. These comprise inorganic acids, bases and salt, and are used as additives in various petroleum products.

Polarimeter

It is an instrument used to measure optical activity.

Polar molecule

It is a type of molecule with a pair of electric charges of opposite polarity such as water, ammonia, etc.

Polarography

In this electrochemical method of chemical analysis, a sample is subjected to electrolysis by means of a special electrode and a variety of applied voltages.

Polaroid

It is a plastic film that generates a high degree of plane polarisation in light passing through it, and is used in sunglasses.

Polonium [Po]

Naturally found in uranium ores, this rare, radioactive metallic element of atomic number 84, its uses include heaters in space probes, antistatic devices, etc.

Poly

It is a prefix indicating the existence of many atoms or groups of a particular kind in a molecule.

Polyacrylamide

Prepared by polymerising acrylamide, this water-soluble, synthetic resin is used for stabilizing gels and also as a thickening ingredient.

Polyamide

Made naturally and artificially, it is a synthetic, fibre-forming polymer in which the structural units are bonded by amide groupings.

Polyatomic molecule

It is a molecule with more than two atoms which are covalently bonded.

Polybasic acid

It is an acid with more than one displaceable hydrogen atom.

Polycyclic

It relates to an organic compound with many rings of atoms in the molecule.

Polyene

It is a compound consisting of more than one double bond per molecule.

Polyester

This light, strong, weather-resistant, synthetic resin, in which the polymer units are linked by ester groups, is used for making synthetic textile fibres, plastics, etc.

Polyethene

This polymerized ethylene resin, also called polythene, is the most widely used plastic in the form of containers, kitchenware, packaging, etc.

Polymer

Occurring naturally and made artificially, it is a compound with a large molecule containing chains of linked monomer units.

Polymerization

It is a chemical process in which the combination of many small molecules form large molecules resulting in a polymer or polymeric compound.

Polymethanal

Obtained by evaporation of a liquid methanol solution, this solid polymer of methanal is used to reduce degradation in cells, tissues, etc.

Polymethylmethacrylate

Formed from the polymerization of methyl methacrylate, this transparent, rigid thermoplastic or synthetic resin, abbreviated as PMMA, is used as a substitute for glass in products.

Polymorphism

It refers to the existence of different kinds of crystal structure of the same chemical substance.

Polyol

This alcohol which has several hydroxyl groups is used to produce other polymers.

Polyproprene

Another name for polypropylene, this thermoplastic polymer of propylene is a synthetic resin made chemically, and is used in textiles, packaging, etc.

Polysaccharides

These are complex carbohydrates whose molecules consist of chains of monosaccharide molecules such as cellulose, starch, dextrin, etc.

Polystyrene

Industrially manufactured from petroleum, this rigid, transparent synthetic resin, which is a polymer of styrene, is used mainly as packing, films, etc.

Polyurethane

This synthetic resin in which the polymer units contain the urethane radical is used mainly as acomponent of paints, adhesives, etc.

Polyvinylacetate [$(C_4H_6O_2)_n$]

Abbreviated as PVA and commonly known as carpenter's glue, it is a colourless, transparent, rubbery synthetic polymer belonging to the polyvinyl esters family, and isused primarily in adhesives.

Polyvinyl alcohol

This colourless, water-soluble, oil-resistant synthetic resin is used in adhesives, eye drops, gloves, etc.

Potash

Also known as potassium carbonate and other salts, it is an alkaline potassium compound often used in fertilizers, cement, fire extinguishers, etc.

Potash alum

It is both a compound (hydrated potassium aluminium sulphate) and a group of compounds (alums).

Potassium [K]

Naturally occurring only in ionic salts and produced commercially as well, this light, soft, reactive, silvery-white metallic element of the alkali metal group of atomic number 19 is used in fertilizers, food items, respiration systems, etc.

Potassium bromide [KBr]

This white, water-soluble, crystalline salt is used as an anticonvulsant, and a veterinary drug.

Potassium carbonate [K_2CO_3]

Made by the absorbent reaction of potassium hydroxide and carbon dioxide, this white, water-soluble, deliquescent salt which is alkaline in solution is used as an additive and in manufacturing of glass, cleansing agents, etc.

Potassium chlorate [$KClO_3$]

This white, crystalline salt consisting of potassium, chlorine and oxygen is used in fireworks, explosives, and is utilized as a disinfectant as well.

Potassium chloride [KCl]

Made of potassium and chlorine, this colourless, metal halide salt with a crystalline structure is used in medicines, food processing, etc.

Potassium chromate [K_2CrO_4]

This yellow-coloured, toxic, water-soluble, crystalline salt is used as a chemical intermediate, textile mordant, etc.

Potassium cyanide [KCN]

This colourless, crystalline, water-soluble, toxic compound, which is similar to sugar in appearance is used in electroplating, photography, gold mining, etc.

Potassium dichromate [$K_2Cr_2O_7$]

Formed by the reaction of potassium chloride and sodium dichromate, this orange-red, crystalline, water-soluble, toxic, corrosive salt, also called chromic acid, is used in dyeing, photography, cement, etc.

Potassium hydroxide [KOH]

Commonly known as caustic potash, this strongly alkaline, colourless, deliquescent substance is used in making soaps, and also as an electrolyte in batteries.

Potassium iodate [KIO_3]

This ionic, odourless, white crystalline powder with oxidising properties is used in iodination of salt, baking, and sometimes in radiation treatment.

Potassium iodide [KI]

This white, crystalline, mildly hygroscopic salt is used for commercial purposes such as in organic synthesis, iodized table salt, etc.

Potassium nitrate [KNO_3]

Naturally occurring as mineral niter and also made artificially, this white crystalline salt, a natural source of nitrogen, is used in fertilizers, gunpowder, etc.

Potassium nitrite [KNO_2]

This colourless or mildly yellow, water-soluble, crystalline powder, which is an ionic salt of potassium and nitrite ions, has strong oxidising properties and is used as an accelerator and in medicines as well.

Potassium sulphate [K_2SO_4]

Also called arcanite, this colourless, non-flammable, water-soluble, crystalline salt is used in making glass, fertilizers, etc.

Potassium sulphide [K_2S]

Another name for potassium sulphuret, it is an inorganic compound. It is a rare, water-soluble, colourless solid, used chiefly in fireworks.

Potentiometric titration

In this method, a change in pH is used to determine and measure the alterations in the voltage of an electrode immersed in the solution that is being titrated.

Praseodymium [Pr]

Naturally occurring in bastnasite or monazite, this soft, yellow-white, ductile, highly reactive, trivalent metallic element of the lanthanide group of atomic number 59 is used as an alloying agent, oxidation catalyst, etc.

Precipitate

It is an insoluble substance produced by mixing in solution the constituent ions of a slightly soluble solution.

Precipitation

It refers to this action of forming a chemical solid by precipitating a substance in a solution or solid.

Pressure

It is the amount of force applied to a unit area of surface indicated by the symbol P, and measured in pascals.

Primary alcohol

It is an alcohol in which the hydroxyl radical is attached to a primary carbon.

Primary voltaic cells

These are non-rechargeable cells in which once the reactants are consumed, and electricity is generated, then no further reaction is possible.

Prismane [C_6H_6]

This polycyclic, saturated hydrocarbon is a valence isomer, in which the six carbon atoms are placed at the corners of a triangular prism.

Product

It is a chemical substance produced as a result of a natural or chemical reaction.

Promoter

It is any component or additive that accelerates the activity or selectivity of a catalyst.

Propane [C_3H_8]

Obtained from petroleum products, this inflammable, colourless hydrocarbon gas of the alkane series is mainly used as a domestic and industrial fuel.

Propanol

Also known as propyl alcohol, it is any of the two isomeric alcohols, which are clear, colourless, peculiar-smelling, volatile liquids, and are used as solvents, etc.

Propellant

It is (i) something that provides thrust, such as explosive mixtures; (ii) a compressed inert gas used to force out the aerosol contents of spray cans.

Propenoate

It is a salt or ester of propenoic acid.

Prepenoic acid

Also known as acrylic acid, this unsaturated, carboxylic, corrosive liquid acid is used in the manufacture of the plastic materials, and also for medical purposes.

Propenonitrile

It is a colourless liquid unsaturated nitrile obtained from propene.

Propylene [C_3H_6]

Derived by cracking petroleum, this flammable unsaturated gaseous hydrocarbon of the alkene series, also called propene, is used in making plastics, films, etc.

Prostaglandin

It is a class of cyclic fatty acid or lipid compounds containing 20 carbon atoms with varying hormone-like effects, and plays an important role in the animal body.

Protactinium [Pa]

Naturally occurring as a decay product of uranium, this short-lived, rare, radioactive metallic element of the actinide series with atomic number 91, is applied mainly in the areas of scientific research.

Protamine

Found in fish sperm, this class of simple proteins, which are small, rich in arginine, is used chiefly for medical purposes.

Protease

This enzyme that catalyzes the breaking down of proteins and peptides is used for medical and surgical purposes.

Protein

Present in meat, eggs, milk, legumes, this class of nitrogenous organic compounds, consisting of polymers of amino acids, is a vital part of all living organisms for growth, tissue-repairing, etc.

Proteolysis

It is the process in which the hydrolysis of proteins or peptides break into amino acids by the action of proteases.

Proton

It is a subatomic particle having a mass of 1.0073 amu and a charge of +1, found in the nuclei of atoms.

Protonic acid

It is an acid that liberates solvated hydrogen ions from a polar solvent.

Prout's hypothesis

It refers to the assumption that hydrogen is the main substance from which the other elements have been created.

Prussic acid

Also known as hydrocyanic acid, it is the colourless, weakly acidic, highly toxic liquid solution of hydrogen cyanide which is used in organic synthesis.

Pseudoaromatic

It refers to a substance that is anti-aromatic, having a ring of atoms consisting of alternating double and single bonds.

Pseudohalogens

These compounds resembling halogens include cyanogen and thiocyanogen.

Ptyalin

It is a kind of amylase secreted in the saliva of humans and other mammals.

Pumice

Formed during explosive volcanic eruptions, it is a very light, porous, pyroclasticigneous rock, used as construction material, abrasive, etc.

Pyranose

It is a cyclic hemiacetal form of a monosaccharide (simple sugar) which contains a six-membered pyran ring.

Pyrazine

This heterocyclic aromatic organic compound in grapes is a vital contributor to the aroma of wines.

Pyridine [C_5H_5N]

Usually obtained from coal tar, it is a colourless, poisonous, volatile, flammable, unpleasant-smelling liquid used mainly as a solvent, reagent, etc.

Pyro

It refers to a compound that is produced or affected by heat or has a fiery colour.

Pyrolysis

It is a thermochemical decomposition of a substance at high temperatures in the absence of oxygen.

Pyrometer

It is an instrument used to measure the infrared radiation and temperature emitted by a body or surface.

Pyrophoric

A pyrophoric substance is liable to ignite spontaneously when exposed to air.

Pyrrole [C_4H_4NH]

Found in bone oil and coal tar, this heterocyclic aromatic compound having a five-membered ring is a weak basic, pleasant-smelling liquid.

❑

Quadrivalent

It refers to an atom having a valence of four.

Quadrupole

It is a system of electric charge containing four equal monopoles, or two equal dipoles, placed close together with alternating polarity.

Quadrupole mass analyser

This type of mass analyser has four circular rods, which are set highly parallel to each other, and is mainly used in mass spectrometry.

Qualitative analysis

It refers to that branch of chemistry, which relates with identifying the components such as elements, functional groups present in a sample.

Quantitative analysis

This chemical analysis deals with ascertaining the amount or percentage of one or more components of a substance.

Quantum

It is the smallest quantity of some physical property that a system can possess according to the quantum theory.

Quantum chemistry

It is a branch of theoretical chemistry concerned with quantum mechanics and quantum field theory to provide an explanation of problems in chemistry.

Quantum jump

It refers to an abrupt alteration from one energy level to another such as the transition of an electron, atom, or molecule from one quantum state to another, with the absorption or emission of a quantum.

Quantum mechanics

It is the mathematical method of treating the motion and interaction of particles on the basis of quantum theory, assuming that the energy of small particles is not infinitely divisible.

Quantum numbers

These numbers describe the energies of electrons in atoms in the dynamics of the quantum system.

Quantum simulation

It is the mathematical modeling of systems of large numbers of molecules by computer studies of relatively small clusters.

Quantum state

It refers to a state of a quantized system defined by a set of quantum numbers.

Quantum theory

Based on the concept of quantum mechanics, it is a theory of matter and energy explaining how energy can only exist at certain levels.

Quantum yield

In a radiation-induced process, it is the number of times that a defined event occurs per photon absorbed by the system.

Quartz

Found in most rocks, this hard, glossy, abundant, white mineral comprising silicon dioxide is used in ceramics, cements, etc.

Quasicrystal

It is an accumulation of molecules (solid material) that is crystal-like in certain properties (made of repeating structural units) but does not have a consistent spatial periodicity.

Quaternary ammonium compounds

It is a class of compounds where a central nitrogen atom is linked to four organic radicals and one acid radical.

Quicklime

Also known as calcium oxide (CaO), this white, caustic, alkaline, crystalline oxide is made by heating limestone, and is used for making cement, paper, etc.

Quinhydrone electrode

It is a type of reversible electrode which has a platinum wire in a saturated solution of quinhydrone, and is used to determine the pH concentration of a solution.

Quinic acid [$C_7H_{12}O_6$]

Derived naturally from plants and also obtained artificially by hydrolysis of chlorogenic acid, this cyclic polyol is a water-soluble, crystalline acid.

Quinine

Obtained from cinchona bark, it is a bitter, white, crystalline compound which has medicinal properties, and is also used in flavouring tonic water.

Quinol

Derived from the reduction of quinone, this colourless, crystalline solid, also called hydroquinone, is used as a reducing agent, antioxidant, etc.

Quinoline [C_9H_7N]

Found in coal tar and bone oil, this colourless, hygroscopic, oily liquid with a distinct smell is used as a solvent, building block, etc.

Quinone

It is a group of aromatic compounds which has two carbonyl functional groups in the same six-membered ring, and is used for medical purposes and also for the manufacturing of hydrogen peroxide on a large scale.

❑

Racemic mixture

Also called racemate, this mixture consists of equal amounts of left and right-handed enantiomers of a chiral substance.

Racemisation

It is the formation of a racemate or partial conversion of one enantiomer into another.

Radial distribution function

It refers to the variation of the atomic density as a function of the distance from one particular atom.

Radiation

It refers to the emission of high energy particles or electromagnetic rays emitted during the nuclear decay processes.

Radiationless decay

It is the decay in which electromagnetic radiation is not emitted and there is a transition of a molecule from an excited state to a lower energy state.

Radical

Generally, a highly reactive species, it is an atom or group of atoms consisting of one or more unpaired electrons.

Radical ion

It is a free radical species that carries an electric charge such as cations and anions.

Radioactive dating

It is a technique of dating ancient objects by ascertaining the ratio of amounts of mother and daughter nuclides present in an object.

Radioactive series

It refers to a chained series of nuclides, each of which changes by radioactive decay into the next until the resultant is a stable nuclide. The first member of the series is the parent, the intermediate members are daughters, and the final member is the end product.

Radioactivity

It is the spontaneous disintegration of atomic nuclei leading to the emission of ionising radiation or particles.

Radiochemistry

This chemistry deals with the radioactive substances.

Radiolysis

It is the process in which the molecular disintegration of a substance by radiation takes place, resulting in change in chemical compounds.

Radium [Ra]

Naturally found in minute amounts in uranium ores, it is a rare, white, strongly oxidising, radioactive metallic element of the alkaline earth series with atomic number 88.

Radium bromide [$RaBr_2$]

This stable yet explosive bromide salt of radium is used in separating radium from uranium ore.

Radon [Rn]

Found as a decay product of uranium, this rare, radioactive, colourless, odourless, gaseous element belonging to the noble gas series, with atomic number 86 is used in the medical and scientific fields.

Raffinose

Naturally found in sugar beets, cotton seeds, and many cereals, this trisaccharide is made of galactose, fructose, and glucose.

Raoult's law

This law states that the vapour pressure of a solvent in an ideal solution decreases as its mole fraction decreases.

Rare-earth elements

It is a class of elements containing the elements in the lanthanides series (atomic numbers 57 through 71).

Rate constant

It is a coefficient of proportionality relating the rate of a reaction to the concentration of reactant in a unimolecular reaction.

Rate-determining step

It is the slowest step in a mechanism or chemical reaction, which determines the overall rate of reaction.

Rate-law expression

It is the equation relating the rate of a reaction to the concentrations of the reactants and the specific rate of the constant.

Rate of reaction

It is the rate or time or speed (fast or slow) a reaction takes in changing the concentration of a reactant or a product in a specific chemical reaction.

Rayon

Produced from regenerated cellulose, this semi-synthetic, silk-like fibre is used mainly in the textile industry.

Reactants

These substances take part in and are consumed in a chemical reaction.

Reaction ratio

It is the relative amounts of reactants and products, which are a part of a reaction.

Reagent

It is a chemical substance or a mixture used for treating materials, samples, or compounds and in chemical reaction as well.

Rearrangement

It is a kind of reaction in which new bonds are formed due to excitation.

Recrystallisation

In this purification process, the impure substance is dissolved in a solvent, and then crystallized to derive a pure substance.

Red phosphorous

This violet-red, non-toxic, amorphous powder is an allotropic form of phosphorus.

Reducing agent

It is the substance that reduces another substance or species by being oxidised and losing electrons.

Reducing sugar

It is any sugar that has the ability to reduce other compounds and has an aldehyde or a ketone group in solution.

Reduction

In this process, electrons are added to an atom along with oxidation of the reducing agent.

Refining

It refers to the process of removing impurities or unwanted elements from a substance, or separating from extraneous matter.

Relative density

It is the ratio of the density of a substance to the density of a standard.

Relative molecular mass

It is the sum of all the relative atomic masses of the constituent atoms of a molecule.

Relaxation

It refers to the restoration of equilibrium following a perturbed system.

Renewable energy sources

These sources of energy can be naturally replenished and are derived from natural resources such as sunlight, wind, rain, etc.

Rennin

This aspartic acid protease enzyme found in the stomach of suckling animals, causes milk to coagulate.

Resin

Naturally found in plants or synthetically prepared by polymerization, this organic polymer is used in plastics, adhesives, varnishes, etc.

Resolution

It is a phenomenon by which a racemic mixture is separated into its two constituent enantiomorphs.

Resonance

It is the concept in which two or more conventional formulas for the same arrangement of atoms are needed for describing the bonding in a molecule.

Resonance ionisation spectroscopy

This spectroscopy is a technique that uses resonant laser excitation, and is capable of detecting single atoms or molecules of an element.

Resorcinol [$C_6H_4(OH)_2$]

Derived from many resins, this crystalline, dihydroxy phenol is used in manufacturing dyes, resins, cosmetics, etc.

Retrosynthetic analysis

This analysis is a method for solving problems in the planning of organic synthesis by working backward.

Reverse osmosis

In this process, pure water is produced by forcing solvent molecules to flow through a semipermable membrane from a concentrated solution into a dilute solution by the application of greater hydrostatic pressure.

Reversible process

In this process, a system can be made to go through the same steps in the reverse order.

Reversible reaction

It is a reaction that can proceed in both the forward and reverse direction, and in which the products can make reagents and reagents can make products.

Rhenium [Re]

Derived in minute amounts from the ores of molybdenum, this rare, heavy, polyvalent, silvery-white metallic element with atomic number 75 is used in alloys, as a catalyst, etc.

Rheopexy

It is a rare property of some non-Newtonian fluids exhibited by some slow-gelling, thixotropic sols of gelling more rapidly when shaken gently.

Rhodium [Rh]

Naturally found in platinum ores, this rare, white, hard, metallic element of the transition series with atomic number 45 is used in alloys, jewellery, etc.

Ribose [$C_5H_{10}O_5$]

It is a pentose sugar that is naturally found as a constituent of nucleosides, vitamins, enzymes, etc.

Ricin

Obtained from castor beans, this highly poisonous protein is used as a chemical and biological warfare reagent, and is researched for its potential use in medicines.

Ring

It is a group of atoms connected by bonds in a circular or triangular form.

Roasting

This metallurgical process in which a sulphide ore is heated in air may lead to the conversion of a metal sulphide to a metal oxide or to a free metal.

Rochelle salt

Also known as a potassium sodium tartrate, this double salt acts as a cathartic and is also used in Seidlitz powder.

Roentgenium [Rg]

Produced artificially, it is a radioactive transuranic element of atomic number 111.

Rose's metal

Another name for rose's alloy, this fusible alloy with a low melting point is made of bismuth, lead and tin and is mainly used as a solder.

Rosin

Obtained from the sap of pine trees, this natural resin is usually used as a flux and in aquatint.

Rotamer

It is any set of isomers of a molecule that can be interconverted by restricted rotation of part of the molecule around a single bond.

Rotaxane

This mechanically-interlocked molecular architecture contains a dumbbell-shaped molecule which is threaded through a ring.

Rubber

Obtained from the latex sap of trees and also synthetically made, this tough, elastic, polymeric substance can be finished into a variety of products such as in textile industry, paper industry, carpet industry, etc.

Rubidium [Rb]

Naturally occurring in minerals (carnallite, lepidolite, pollucite), this rare, soft silvery-white, reactive metallic element of the alkali metal group with atomic number 37 is used in fireworks, for laser cooling, medicines, etc.

Ruby

This transparent, precious stone containing corundum in different colours (from purple to pale rose) is used as a gemstone and in lasers.

Rusting

It is the formation of reddish-brown corrosion product on iron by low-temperature oxidation due to the presence of moisture.

Ruthenium [Ru]

This rare, hard, silvery-white, polyvalent metallic element of the transition series with atomic number 44 is used as a plating material, catalyst, etc.

Rutherfordium [Rf]

Produced artificially by high-energy atomic collisions, it is an unstable element with atomic number 104.

Rutile

Occurring as needle like crystals, this reddish-brown mineral consists of titanium dioxide in crystalline form, is a major source of titanium.

❑

Saccharin [$C_7H_5NO_3S$]

Used mainly as a substitute for sugar, this white, crystalline, sweet-tasting powder is used as an artificial sweetener in food and drinks.

Sal ammoniac

Made chiefly of ammonium chloride, this rare, brittle, soft mineral which is found in different colours (white to yellow) is used as a flux, flavouring agent, etc.

Salicyclic acid [$C_6H_4(OH)(COOH)$]

Found in certain plants, this white, crystalline, bitter-tasting substance is used in organic synthesis, in the production of aspirin and other industrial chemicals.

Saline

This solution consists of sodium chloride or magnesium salts with distilled water.

Salinometer

It is a hydrometer for determining the salinity of a solution.

Sal soda

This hydrated sodium carbonate, a sodium salt of carbonic acid, is used in the manufacture of cleaning solutions such as soap powders, etc.

Salt bridge

This instrument has a U-shaped tube containing electrolyte, which links the oxidation and reduction half-cells of a voltaic cell.

Salt cake

Derived as a by product in several industrial processes, this anhydrous, impure form of sodium sulphate is used mainly in the sulphate process for wood pulp, in the manufacture of detergents, glass, etc.

Samarium [Sm]

Naturally occurring in minerals (monazite, bastnasite), this hard, silvery-grey, lustrous metallic element of the lanthanide series with atomic number 62 has many uses in metallic alloys, ceramics, glazes, etc.

Sandmeyer reaction

This chemical reaction is used preparing aryl halides from aryl diazonium salts as catalysts.

Sanger's reagent

Applied in structural protein chemistry, this chemical is used for polypeptide sequencing in which the sequence of amino acids is determined.

Saponification

In this process, the hydrolysis of esters occurs in the presence of a strong soluble base or an alkali.

Saponin

Found in several plant species, this toxic compound forms foam when shaken with water, and is used in detergents, foaming agents, etc.

Sapphire

This variety of corundum (aluminum oxide) is a transparent, blue-coloured, precious stone, which is used mainly in jewellery.

Sarin [$(CH_3)_2CHO$]$CH_3P(O)F$]

It is an organophosphorus, highly poisonous, colourless, odourless compound which is used as a chemical weapon.

Saturated hydrocarbons

Also called alkanes or paraffin hydrocarbons, these hydrocarbons contain only single bonds.

Saturated solution

It is a solution in which no more solute will dissolve.

Saturation spectroscopy

This branch of spectroscopy is used to assess and analyse atomic and molecular structure, and to determine accurate values for physical constants.

S-block elements

These elements in the periodic table comprise the alkali metals and alkaline earth metals, along with hydrogen and helium.

Scandium [Sc]

Derived from some uranium ores, this soft, silvery-white, trivalent metallic element of atomic number 21 is used mainly in making aerospace components.

Scavenger

This chemical agent is added to a chemical mixture for the removal of impurities or unwanted products.

Schiff base

Derived from the condensation of aldehydes with primary amines, this colourless crystalline compound contains a carbon-nitrogen double bond, and is used as chemical intermediates and perfume bases, etc.

Schiff's reagent

This aqueous solution of rosaniline and sulphurous acid is used chiefly for detecting aldehydes in Schiff's test.

Seaborgium [Sg]

Produced artificially by high-energy atomic collisions, it is a very unstable, transuranic element of atomic number 106.

Sebacic acid [$C_{10}H_{18}O_4$]

Derived from castor oil, this non-toxic, dicarboxylic acid is used in plasticizers, cosmetics, antiseptics, etc.

Secondary alcohol

It refers to a class of alcohols containing the radical CH.OH bonded with two hydrocarbon radicals.

Secondary amine

It is an amine containing two radicals (R1R2-NH), where R1 and R2 stand for either similar or different groups.

Secondary cell

It is a rechargeable voltaic cell, in which original reactants can be regenerated by reversing the direction of the electric current.

Second-order reaction

In this reaction, the reaction rate is proportional to the concentration of each of two reacting molecules or chemical species.

Sedimentation

It is a method in which heavier, suspended matter is separated from a liquid solution, and is used for measuring the size of large molecules.

Seed

This small single crystal acts as a nucleus for crystallization and is used for developing a larger crystal from a saturated crystal solution.

Selenide

It is a binary compound of divalent selenium with a more electropositive element.

Selenium [Se]

Occurring in several allotropic forms, this grey, toxic, crystalline non-metallic element of atomic number 34 is used in alloys, glass production, etc.

Selenium cell

This solar cell is a photoelectric device which consists of a strip of selenium and generates electric current according to the intensity of light.

Self-organisation

It is the ability of a system to create a well-defined molecular entity spontaneously by organizing from components in a particular condition.

Seliwanoff's test

This colour test is used for the identification of aldose and ketose sugars.

Semicarbazones

It is a product obtained from condensation reaction between a ketone or aldehyde and semicarbazide.

Semiconductor

It is a substance (germanium, silicon, etc.) with electrical properties intermediate between a good conductor and a good insulator, and as the temperature rises its conductivity increases.

Semi-empirical calculations

It is a method related to the study large molecular systems, in which the atomic and molecular quantities are calculated.

Semimetal

These substances have properties of both metals and non-metals such as antimony, cobalt, zinc, etc.

Semipermable membrane

It is a thin partition between two solutions through which certain molecules (based on size and charge) can pass but others cannot.

Septivalent

Also known as heptavalent, it is something which has a valency of seven.

Sequestration

It is the ability to react with potentially troublesome metal ions to form stable coordination complexes.

Sesquiterpene [$C_{15}H_{24}$]

This class of terpenes, acyclic or with rings, consists of three isoprene units and is used as an antiseptic, a calming agent, etc.

Shale

Formed by the deposition of layers of mud or clay, it is a soft, grey-coloured, fine-grained sedimentary rock which can easily disintegrate into slabs.

Shellac

Naturally found as secretion of the lac insect on trees, this resin is processed and made into thin dry flakes and is used in the production of varnishes, glazes, etc.

Shock wave

It is a sudden alteration of pressure in a narrow region travelling through a liquid or gas at a velocity greater than that of sound.

Side chain

It is a group of atoms that is linked to the main chain (core part of the molecule) and has a ring or chain structure.

Side reaction

It is a secondary reaction which takes place at the same time with the main chemical reaction and diminishes the yield of the end product.

Sigma bond

It is a covalent bond which is a result of the head-on overlap of atomic orbitals, in which the area of electron sharing is symmetrical to the axis linking the two bonded atoms.

Sigmatropic reaction

In this pericyclic reaction, the net result is one σ-bond is changed to another σ-bond in a process which involves a single molecule and does not use a catalyst.

Silane

It is (i) a colourless, flammable gaseous compound (SiH_4) comprising silicon and hydrogen, also called monosilane, which has strong reducing properties; (ii) any of the group of hydrides of silicon analogous to the alkanes.

Silica gel

Prepared artificially from sodium silicate, this hard, granular, hygroscopic, porous form of silica is used as a desiccant, stationary phase, etc.

Silicate

It is a salt or ester obtained from silicic acid.

Silicide

This binary compound of silicon with a more electropositive element or radical is mainly used as contacts to silicon and conductors.

Silicon [Si]

Present in both crystalline form and as an amorphous powder, this abundant, tetravalent non-metallic element of atomic number 14 is used as a semiconductor in electronic products such as circuits, transistors, etc.

Silicon carbide [SiC]

Naturally found as the rare mineral moissanite, this hard, refractory, blue-black, crystalline compound of silicon and carbon, also called carborundum, is used as an abrasive, a heat refractory material, etc.

Silicon dioxide [SiO]

Naturally occurring as quartz, sand and opal, this colourless, hard, vitreous, insoluble solid, commonly known as silica, is used to produce elemental silicon.

Silicon hydride

It is a class of inorganic silicon-hydrogen compounds with covalent bonds.

Siloxanes

Belonging to the organosilicon class of compounds, these compounds have a molecular structure based on a chain of alternate silicon and oxygen atoms.

Silver [Ag]

Naturally occurring in argentite and also in free form, this precious, soft, shiny, greyish-white, univalent metallic element of atomic number 47, is used in coins, jewellery, photography, etc.

Silver bromide [AgBr]

This bromideis a soft, pale-yellow, water insoluble salt that darkens when exposed to light, and is used in making photographic emulsions.

Silver chloride [AgCl]

This colourless, insoluble powder or solid that darkens when exposed to light is used in the manufacture of photographic emulsions, papers, etc.

Silver nitrate [$AgNO_3$]

This nitrate is a water-soluble, colourless solid, which is sensitive to light, and is used in photographic emulsions, in medicine, etc.

Silver oxide [Ag_2O]

Prepared by combining silver nitrate solutions with a base, this fine dark brown powder is used in making silver-oxide batteries, other silver compounds, etc.

Sima

Named after the two main chemical constituents, silica and magnesia, it is a rock material that forms the lower layer of the earth's oceanic crust.

Singlet

It is an electronic state of an atom or a molecule in which all spins are paired.

Sintered glass

Prepared by sintering glass powder, it is a porous glass which is used in the fields of pharmacy research, biotechnology, etc.

SI units

Known as Standard International units, it is a specific system of metric units for measuring physical quantities such as length, volume, temperature, etc.

Smelting

It is a kind of extractive metallurgical operation, which is used to produce a metal after it is separated by fusion from its ores.

Soap

Prepared from fats and sodium hydroxide, this substance can mix with both water and oil, and is typically used as a cleansing agent.

Soda

It refers to any of several forms of sodium carbonate (Na_2CO_3).

Soda ash

Another name for sodium carbonate, this commercially manufactured anhydrous form is used in making soap powders, glass, paper, etc.

Sodamide [$NaNH_2$]

Also known as sodium amide, this white (pure form), highly reactive solid is used in the industrial production of indigo, hydrazine, etc.

Sodium [Na]

Found in natural compounds (sea water and minerals), this soft, waxy, silver-white, reactive metallic element of the alkali metal group with atomic number 11 is used as a heat transfer fluid, desiccant, reducing agent, etc.

Sodium aluminate [$NaAlO_2$]

Prepared by the dissolution of aluminium hydroxide in a caustic soda solution, this commercial inorganic crystalline compound is used for many industrial purposes.

Sodium azide [NaN_3]

Obtained from the Wislicenus process, this colourless, ionic, toxic, water-soluble salt is used in automobile airbags, in the manufacturing of azide compounds, etc.

Sodium bromide [NaBr]

This high-melting, colourless, bitter-tasting, crystalline salt of bromine is used in the pharmaceutical and petroleum industry, as disinfectant, etc.

Sodium carbonate [Na_2CO_3]

This sodium salt of carbonic acid is a colourless, water-soluble, powdery compound is used in the production of glass, ceramics, detergents, soap, etc.

Sodium chloride [NaCl]

Found in nature (seawater and halite), this white, ionic, crystalline substance consisting mainly of sodium chloride, also called common salt, is commonly used as a condiment and food preservative, and for many industrial applications.

Sodium cyanide [NaCN]

Obtained from neutralization reactions, this colourless, toxic, crystalline, soluble salt is used in case-hardening steel, electroplating, gold mining, etc.

Sodium fluoride [NaF]

A source of the fluoride ion, this white, ionic, crystalline salt of sodium is used to fluoridate water, in toothpastes, as a cleaning agent, etc.

Sodium hydride [NaH]

Made by reacting hydrogen and liquid sodium, this inflammable, grey-coloured, crystalline binary compound is mainly used as a strong base in organic synthesis.

Sodium iodide [NaI]

Prepared from the reaction of iodine and sodium hydroxide, this colourless, crystalline salt is used in radiation detection, iodine deficiency treatment, etc.

Sodium monoxide [Na_2O]

This strong, basic, colourless granular material, which when treated with water forms sodium hydroxide, is used in the manufacture of ceramics, glasses, etc.

Sodium nitrate [$NaNO_3$]

This naturally occurring, colourless, water-soluble, powdery salt is used mainly in the production of nitric acid, fertilizers, explosives, etc.

Sodium peroxide [Na_2O_2]

Obtained by burning sodium and oxygen, this yellow-white, water-soluble solid is a strong base with oxidising properties.

Sodium sesquicarbonate [$Na_3H(CO_3)_2$]

This mixed salt of sodium bicarbonate and sodium carbonate with a needle-like crystal structure is used in bath salts, conserving archeological objects, etc.

Sodium sulphate [Na_2SO_4]

This sodium salt of sulphuric acid is a colourless, bitter, crystalline solid, which is used in making glass, paper, dyes, medicines, etc.

Sodium sulphide [Na_2S]

Prepared by heating sodium sulphate with coal, this yellow to red, water-soluble solid is used mainly in the paper industry, and also as a reducing agent and solvent.

Sodium thiosulphate [$Na_2S_2O_3$]

Also called hypo, this white, soluble, crystalline compound is used in photographic developing, extracting gold, in medicines, etc.

Soft water

This form of water does not contain mineral salts (calcium or magnesium), and allows the formation of lather with soap.

Sol

It is a fluid suspension of a colloidal solid in a liquid.

Solder

This low-melting, fustible metal alloy is used in joining metallic surfaces (soldering), electronics, plumbing, etc.

Solubility

It is the amount of a substance that can dissolve in a particular solvent.

Solubility product

It is a kind of dynamic equilibrium for a reaction, where a solid ionic compound dissolves to yield its ions in a saturated solution.

Solute

It is the dispersed or dissolved phase of a solution.

Solution

It is a homogeneous mixture of two or more substances.

Solvation

In this process, the solvent molecules surround and interact with solute molecules.

Solvent

It is the dispersing medium of a solution.

Solvolysis

It is the chemical reaction of a substance with the solvent in which it is dissolved.

Sonochemistry

This branch of chemistry is related to understanding the effect of ultrasonic energy (sonic waves and wave properties) on chemical systems.

Sorbitol

Made by the reduction of glucose, this sugar alcohol is a sweet-tasting, crystalline compound, which is also known as glucitol, and is used as an artificial sweetener.

Sorption

It is the accumulation of molecules of a substance by another in a different phase.

Species

It is a set of chemically identical structural entities or units (atom, molecule, or ion) in a solid array.

Specific gravity

It is the ratio of the density of a substance to the density of reference substance.

Spectrochemical series

It is an arrangement of ligands in order of increasing ligand field strength.

Spectrometer

It is an instrument used for recording and measuring spectra (wavelengths of light).

Spectroscope

It is an instrument used for producing and recording spectra by splitting it up into its component colours.

Sphalerite

This chief ore of zinc is a shiny, crystalline mineral in different colours (yellow to dark brown or black), containing mainly zinc sulphide and variable iron.

Spiegel

It is a lustrous, crystalline pig iron which has large quantities of manganese and is used as a deoxidising agent and in steel manufacturing.

Spinel [$MgAl_2O_4$]

Occurring as octahedral crystals in many colours, this hard, glassy, mineral which is a magnesium aluminium member of the spinel group, is used as gemstones.

Spiro compound

It is a polycyclic organic compound with rings linked through just one atom called spiroatom, which is usually carbon.

Spontaneous combustion

This slow process refers to the ignition of an organic substance without an external ignition source, which usually results from an internal oxidation process.

Spot test

Used for quality assurance, it is a test of material density and modulus at the chosen spots.

Sputtering

In this process, there is an accumulation of metal on a surface by using fast ions to eject particles of it from a target. It is used for thin-film deposition, etching, etc.

Squalene

Naturally occurring in plants, animals and humans, it is an oily liquid compound which is a metabolic precursor of sterols.

Square-planar

It is a term used to describe molecules and polyatomic ions that have one atom in the centre and four atoms at the corners of a square.

Stabilizer

Called an antonym to a catalyst, this chemical has a tendency of inhibiting the reaction between two or more other chemicals.

Stainless steel

Also called inox steel, this form of steel consists of chromium, which makes it resistant to staining, tarnishing and corrosion.

Stalactites and stalagmites

Naturally occurring in limestone caves, these are mineral deposits, usually of calcite or aragonite, in a conical or cylindrical form.

Standard electrode potential

Abbreviated as E° or Eo, it is the measure of individual potential of a reversible electrode under standard conditions.

Stannate

It is (i) a salt of stannic acid; (ii) the compounds of tin.

Starch

Found in natural sources (seeds, cereals, etc.), this odourless, tasteless, colourless polysaccharide functions as a complex carbohydrate, which is a vital foodstuff, and is used in adhesives, paper and textile industry as well.

Steam distillation

It is a kind of separation process of a liquid in a current of steam, which is used to separate botanical matter from essential oils that are immiscible with water.

Stearate [$C_{17}H_{35}COO^-$]

It is the anion form or salt of stearic acid.

Stearic acid [$C_{18}H_{36}O_2$]

Derived from animal or vegetable fats, this solid, waxy, water-soluble, saturated fatty acid, also called octadecanoic acid, is used as a thickener and co-emulsifier.

Steel

Consisting mainly of iron and carbon, this hard, strong, grey-coloured alloy is used mainly as a structural and fabricating material such as in construction, etc.

Stereochemistry

This branch of chemistry is related to the three-dimensional spatial arrangements of atoms within molecules, and its effects on the properties of molecules.

Steric effect

It refers to the spatial arrangement of molecules influencing reacting substances.

Steric hindrance

It is the prevention or retardation of chemical reaction due to the spatial structure of a molecule.

Steroid

It is a group of fat-soluble organic compounds with four rings of carbon atoms, which include hormones, alkaloids that help control important functions.

Stoichiometry

It is a description of the quantitative relationships among elements and compounds as they undergo chemical changes.

Stopped-flow technique

It is a method for investigating fast reactions in solution, mainly for reactions occurring in the millisecond time range.

Strong acid

This acid completely dissociates in an aqueous solution with the loss of one proton.

Strontium [Sr]

Occurring in celestite and strontianite, this soft, silver-white or yellow metallic element of the alkaline earth series with atomic number 38 is used in fireworks, flares, nuclear reactors, magnets, etc.

Structural formula

It is a kind of molecular notation that shows the arrangement of atoms in the molecule of a compound.

Styrene

Derived as a petroleum byproduct, this unsaturated, colourless, oily, sweet-smelling, liquid hydrocarbon, also known as vinyl benzene, is used in the manufacture of polymers, plastics, etc.

Sublimation

It is the direct vapourization of a solid by heating without becoming liquid.

Substituent

It is an atom or group of atoms substituted in the place of another atom or group or being in a particular position in a molecule.

Substitution reaction

It is a reaction in which an atom or a group of atoms is replaced by another atom or group of atoms.

Succinic acid [$C_4H_6O_4$]

Derived from amber, this colourless, crystalline, dicarboxylic acid, also called butanedioic acid, plays an important role in the metabolic Krebs cycle.

Sucrose

Obtained from many plants, this colourless, odourless, sweet-tasting, crystalline powder, sometimes called saccharose, is mainly used as a sweetening agent.

Sugar

Found in many plants, this class of sweet-tasting, edible crystalline carbohydrates, mainly containing sucrose, is used as a sweetener in food and drinks.

Sulphamic acid [H_3NSO_3]

Prepared by the reaction of sulphuric acid, sulphur trioxide and urea, this colourless, water-soluble, strong crystalline acid, also called amidosulphuric acid, is used as a catalyst, dye, herbicide, coagulator, etc.

Sulphanilic acid [$C_6H_7NO_3S$]

Made by sulphonation of aniline, this off-white, crystalline solid with a high melting point is used as a dye and also as a standard in combustion analysis.

Sulphate

It is a salt or ester of sulphuric acid.

Sulphides

These are binary compounds of sulphur with another element or group which is more electropositive.

Sulphinic acid

It is an oxoacid of sulphur having the structure RS(=O)OH, in which the sulphur is oxidised by addition of two oxygen atoms.

Sulphite

It is a compound containing the sulphite ion SO_3^{2-}, which is used as a food preservative such as protecting wine from oxidation and bacterial activity.

Sulphonate

It is a salt or ester of a sulponic acid.

Sulphonation

In this chemical reaction, there is a formation of sulphonic acid when a–SO_3H group is substituted on a benzene ring.

Sulphonic acid

It is any of various organic acids derived from sulphuric acid.

Sulphur [S]

Naturally occurring in several sulphide and sulphate minerals, this yellow-coloured, abundant, odourless, multivalent, crystalline non-metallic element of atomic number 16 is used for making fertilizers, pharmaceuticals, etc.

Sulphur dioxide [SO_2]

Naturally found in volcanoes and produced in industrial processes, this colourless, toxic gas is used as a preservative, reducing agent, refrigerant, etc.

Sulphuric acid [H_2SO_4]

Derived from sulphur dioxide, this colourless, strong, water-soluble, extremely corrosive acid is mainly used as an electrolyte, catalyst, cleaning agent, etc.

Sulphurous acid [H_2SO_3]

Formed by the dissolution of sulphur dioxide in water, this unstable weak acid is used as a reducing and bleaching agent.

Superacid

It is a solution of a strong acid in a non-aqueous acidic solvent.

Supercooling

Another name for undercooling, it is lowering the temperature of a liquid or a gas below its freezing point, without actually obtaining the transformation.

Superheating

Sometimes called boiling delay, it is the process in which a liquid is heated to a temperature higher than its boiling point without its vapourization.

Superoxides

These are metallic oxides with the univalent anion O_2^-.

Supersaturation

It is a solution consisting of a higher than saturation concentration of solute which is usually not possible.

Surfactant

Functioning as a wetting agent, this substance reduces the surface tension of a liquid in which the dissolution takes place.

Suspension

It is a heterogeneous mixture in which solid particles settle out of fluid-like phase.

Syneresis

It is the extraction of a liquid from a gel by contraction.

Synthesis

It is the process of forming a chemical compound or a product by uniting and reacting of simpler chemical compounds.

Synthetic

It is a compound or product prepared artificially by chemical reactions.

❑

Tabun [$C_5H_{11}N_2O_2P$]

This organophosphorus nerve gas is a toxic, combustible, clear, colourless liquid is used as a chemical warfare agent.

Tactic polymer

It is a polymer with regularity in the structural configuration of its molecules.

Talc

Found as translucent masses or laminae, this soft, fine-grained mineral in various colours with a soap-like feel comprising hydrated magnesium silicate is used in several products such as talcum powder, plastics, paints, etc.

Tannic acid [$C_{76}H_{52}O_{46}$]

Derived from nutgalls, this polyphenol is a white or yellow-coloured substance with weak acidity and is used in tanning, textiles, etc.

Tannin

Naturally occurring in plants, this yellow brown, bitter-tasting, polyphenolic substance, containing derivatives of gallic acid, is used in the manufacture of leather, inks, medicines, etc.

Tantalum [Ta]

Occurring naturally in minerals (niobite, fergusonite and tantalite), this rare, hard, silver-grey, lustrous, corrosion-resistant metallic element of the transition series of atomic number 73 is used in electronics, alloys, etc.

Tar

Obtained by destructive distillation of wood or coal, this dark, thick, flammable liquid comprises a mixture of hydrocarbons, resins, and other compounds, it is used in making roads, preserving timber, etc.

Tartaric acid [$C_4H_6O_6$]

Naturally found in several fruits, this colourless, crystalline, diprotic organic acid is used in soft drinks, baking powder, confectionaries, etc.

Tartrate

It is a salt or ester of tartaric acid.

Tartrazine

Obtained from tartaric acid, this lemon-yellow, water-soluble, synthetic dye is used to colour food, drugs, cosmetics, etc.

Tautomerism

It is a form of structural isomerism where the two isomers are in equilibrium.

Technetium [Tc]

Derived synthetically as one of the fission products of uranium, it is acrystalline, radioactive metallic element of atomic number 43.

Tellurides

It is abinary compound of tellurium with other more electropositive elements.

Tellurium [Te]

Found chiefly as tellurides in ores (copper, nickel, silver and gold), this brittle, shiny, mildly toxic, silvery-white semimetallic element of atomic number 52 is used in some electrical devices, alloys, etc.

Temperature

It is a measure of the intensity of heat (the hotness or coldness) of a substance.

Tempering

It is a heat treatment method for metals, alloys and glass to improve their hardness and elasticity.

Temporary hardness

Commonly called carbonate hardness, it refers to the hardness in water because of the presence of calcium and magnesium carbonates and bicarbonates which can be removed by heating.

Terbium [Tb]

Naturally occurring in minerals (apatite, monazite, xenotime and ytterbite), this rare, ductile, soft, malleable, silvery-white metallic element of the lanthanide series of atomic number 65 is chiefly used in semiconductors, lasers, etc.

Terephthalic acid[$C_6H_4(COOH)_2$]

Prepared synthetically by oxidation of p-xylene by oxygen in air, this colourless, crystalline organic acid, which is one of three isomeric phthalic acids, is used mainly in the manufacture of polyester resins and other polymers.

Ternary compound

It is a compound containing three elements, and may be ionic or covalent.

Terpenes

Found mainly in plants (conifers and trees), it is a class of volatile unsaturated hydrocarbons ($C_{10}H_{16}$), which is used in perfume, food flavours, rubber, etc.

Terpinenes

These cyclicterpenes ($C_{10}H_{16}$) are present in three isomeric forms and are used in perfumes and food flavouring.

Tertiary alcohol

It is a trisubstituted alcohol in which a carbon atom is holding the hydroxyl group and attached by its other three valences to other carbon atoms in a ring.

Tervalent

Another name for trivalent, it is something having a valence of three.

Tetrachloroethene [C_2Cl_4]

Also called tetrachloroethylene, this non-flammable, colourless, synthetically produced liquid is used for dry-cleaning fabrics, making other chemicals, etc.

Tetrachloromethane [CCl_4]

Another name for carbon tetrachloride, this colourless, non-flammable, volatile, pleasant-smelling liquid is mainly used as a solvent for oils.

Tetradecanoic acid [$C_{14}H_{28}O_2$]

Found in animal and vegetable fats, this saturated fatty acid, commonly known as myristic acid, has its use in medicines, cosmetics, etc.

Tetrahedral compound

It is a compound where four atoms or groups placed at the corners of a tetrahedron are connected by covalent bonds to an atom at the centre.

Tetrahydrocannabinol

Abbreviated as THC, this crystalline compound is the main psychoactive substance present in the cannabis plant.

Tetrahydrofuran

Abbreviated as THF, this colourless, water-soluble, heterocyclic compound is used mainly as a solvent and intermediate.

Thallium [Tl]

Occurring naturally in zinc blende and some iron ores, this soft, silvery-white, toxic, malleable metallic element of atomic number 81 is used in electronics, optics, medicines, etc.

Theobromine

Derived from cacao seeds, this bitter, volatile alkaloid, also known as xantheose, is a mild stimulant resembling caffeine.

Theophylline

Obtained naturally from tea leaves, this bitter, colourless, crystalline compound is used as a drug for the treatment of respiratory diseases such as asthma, etc.

Thermal analysis

In this analysis, the physical and chemical properties of materials or samples are monitored as they change with temperature.

Thermal cracking

It refers to the decomposition by heating a substance in the presence of a catalyst and in the absence of air.

Thermal equilibrium

It refers to a state in which all parts of a system are at the same temperature, which are unchanging in time and uniform in space.

Thermochemistry

It is the branch of chemistry related to the quantities of heat generated or absorbed during chemical reactions and physical transformations.

Thermodynamics

It is the study of the energy transfers accompanying physical and chemical processes.

Thermolysis

Also called thermal decomposition, it is the chemical breakdown of molecules caused by the action of heat.

Thermometer

It is a device for measuring and indicating temperature.

Thermonuclear energy

It is the heat energy released or generated from nuclear fusion reactions.

Thermostat

It is a device that automatically regulates temperature by starting or stopping the supply of heat to maintain the temperature at a desired setting.

Thiazole [C_3H_3NS]

Composed of sulphur and nitrogen, this pale-yellow, synthetic, heterocyclic compound with a disagreeable smell contains a ring of three carbon atoms, sulphur and a nitrogen atom.

Thiols

Sometimes referred to as mercaptans, these are an organosulphur compounds containing the group -SH, and are the sulphur-containing analogue of an alcohol.

Thiosulphuric acid [$H_2S_2O_3$]

Obtained from sulphuric acid by replacement of one oxygen atom by a sulphur atom, this unstable acid is known only in solution or as salts and esters.

Thorium [Th]

Occurring naturally as thorite and monazite sands, and also as a byproduct of uranium decay, this soft, white, tetravalent, radioactive metallic element of the actinide series with atomic number 90 is used mainly in nuclear reactors.

Thulium [Tm]

Found in minerals (monazite, apatite and xenotime), this rare, soft, silvery metallic element of the lanthanide series with atomic number 69 is used as an active laser medium, and is also used in X-ray machines.

Thymol [$C_{10}H_{14}O$]

Found in oil of thyme, this white, crystalline, pleasant-smelling compound is used as a preservative, antiseptic and also in perfumes and flavourings.

Tin [Sn]

Derived mainly from cassiterite, this silvery, malleable, ductile, corrosion-resistant metallic element of atomic number 50 is used in many alloys, tin plating, etc.

Tin chloride

It can refer to (i) stannous chloride ($SnCl_2$): a white crystalline substance which is used as a reducing agent; (ii) stannic chloride ($SnCl_4$): a colourless liquid with a pungent odour which is used as a chemical weapon.

Tin oxide [SnO_2]

Found naturally as the mineral cassiterite, this compound of tin and oxygen, also called stannous oxide, is used for making enamels, for polishing glass, etc.

Tin sulphide

It can refer to (i) tin (II) sulphide (SnS): a naturally occurring compound of tin and sulphur; (ii) tin (IV) sulphide (SnS_2): a naturally occurring, bronze-coloured, crystalline compound known as mosaic gold.

Titanium [Ti]

Found in minerals (rutile and ilmenite), this light, hard, grey, lustrous, corrosion-resistant metallic element of the transition series with atomic number 22, is used in strong lightweight alloys, medicines, jewellery, etc.

Titanium chloride

It can refer to (i) titanium (II) chloride ($TiCl_2$): a black-coloured, highly reactive substance which is a reducing agent; (i) titanium (III) chloride ($TiCl_3$): one of the most common halides of titanium, which is an important catalyst.

Titanium oxide [TiO_2]

Found naturally as the mineral rutile, this white, non-reactive solid, also called titania, is used mainly as a white pigment, and also in paints, food colouring, etc.

Titration

It is a process in which one solution is added to another solution until the reaction between the two solutes is complete.

Top az

This silicate mineral of aluminium and flourine is a precious stone in variety of colours (white, yellow or pale blue) is used mainly as a gemstone in jewellery.

Total ionic equation

It is an equation for a chemical reaction written to display the predominant form of all species in aqueous solution.

Trace element

It is a chemical element present only in small quantities in a particular substance or environment.

Transactinide elements

Known as the super-heavy elements, these are the chemical elements with atomic numbers greater than those of the actinides (103).

Transamination

Also called aminotransfer, it is the transfer of an amino group within a chemical compound such as from an amino acid to a keto acid.

Transition state

This state in chemical reaction is the highest energy along the reaction coordinate.

Transmutation

It is the process in which a substance is changed from one state into another.

Transport number

Another name for transference number, it is a fraction of the total current carried by a particular ion in an electrolyte.

Transuranic elements

These are radioactive elements with an atomic number greater than 92.

Trichloroethene [C_2HCl_3]

Also known as trichloroethylene, it is a clear, stable, non-flammable, pleasant-smelling liquid is used as an industrial solvent, and in other industrial applications.

Trichloromethane [$CHCl_3$]

Commonly known as chloroform, this volatile, colourless, sweet-smelling, dense liquid was formerly used as an anesthetic, and presently as a solvent and reagent.

Triiodomethane [CHI_3]

Generally called iodoform, this pale yellow, volatile, crystalline solid with a strong smell is used mainly as a disinfectant.

Trinitrotoluene [$C_6H_2(NO_2)_3CH_3$]

Derived from the reaction of nitric acid and toluene, it is an extremely explosive, yellow crystalline compound which is widely known as TNT.

Tungsten [W]

Occurring naturally in several ores (wolframite and scheelite), this hard, heavy, steel-grey metallic element of the transition series with atomic number 74, also called wolfram, is used mainly in electrical applications.

Turpentine

Derived from the distillation of turpentine oleoresin, this volatile, pungent oil is used in mixing paints and varnishes, in medicines and as a solvent as well.

Turquoise

Composed of copper aluminum phosphate, this blue-to-green mineral is an opaque, rare, precious stone used chiefly as an ornamental stone in jewellery.

Tyndall effect

Another name for Tyndall scattering, it refers to the phenomenon in which scattering of light (mainly blue) by colloidal particles in its path takes place.

❑

Ultrahigh frequency

Also called the decimeter band, these are a range of electromagnetic waves with frequencies between 300 MHz and 3,000 MHz.

Ultramicroscope

This system of illumination is an optical microscope used to detect and view minute particles, which cannot be seen under an ordinary microscopes, by the use of scattered light.

Ultrasonics

It is related to the science and application of ultrasonic waves and vibrations with a frequency above 20,000 hertz.

Ultraviolet radiation

It is an electromagnetic radiation with a wavelength shorter than that of visible light, but longer than X-rays.

UV-visible spectroscopy

It refers to absorption spectroscopy in the ultraviolet-visible spectral region.

Unimolecular reation

It is a chemical reaction which has only one molecular species (reactant).

Unit cell

It is the smallest group of atoms of a substance with the symmetry of a crystal, and from which the lattice can be generated by repetition in three dimensions.

Univalent

Also called monovalent, it is something having a valence of 1.

Unsaturated compound

It is an organic compound with carbon atoms connected by double or triple bonds.

Unsaturated hydrocarbons

These are hydrocarbons that have double or triple carbon-carbon bonds.

Uraninite

Found in pegmatite dykes, this radioactive mineral in different colours (black, grey, or brown) consists chiefly of uranium oxide.

Uranium [U]

Occurring naturally in the earth's crust, thisheavy, dense, toxic, silvery-grey radioactive metallic element in the actinide series with atomic number 92 is used for nuclear fuels and weapons.

Uranium hexafluoride [UF_6]

This silver-grey, crystalline, poisonous uranium compound is used mainly to enrich the uranium for generating fuel for nuclear reactors.

Uranium oxides

It can refer to any of the compounds of uranium and oxygen such as uranium dioxide (UO_2), uranium trioxide (UO_3), triuranium octoxide (U_3O_8), and uranyl peroxide (UO_4).

Uranium series

Also called uranium decay series, it is the series of nuclides that begins with uranium-238 and proceeds by radioactive decay to lead-206, including isotopes of uranium, thorium, protactinium, radium, radon, etc.

Urethane resins

Another name for polyurethanes, these are polymers with free isocyanate groups are created from the reaction of diisocyanates and an amine, a phenol ora carboxylic compound.

Uric acid [$C_5H_4N_4O_3$]

Found in the blood and urine, this colourless, odourless, insoluble compound is a breakdown product of nitrogenous metabolism.

❑

Vacuum

It is a volume of space in which matter is absent, and its gaseous pressure is much less than atmospheric pressure.

Vacuum distillation

It is a technique in which distillation of a liquid takes place under reduced vapour pressure, leading to the evaporation of liquids with the lowest boiling points.

Valence electrons

These are the outermost electrons of atoms, which are generally involved in bonding.

Vanadium [V]

Occurring in several minerals (carnotite and vanadinite), this soft, toxic, grey, ductile metallic element of the transition series with atomic number 23 is used in the manufacture of special alloy steels.

Vanadium oxide

It can refer to any of the compounds of vanadium and oxygen such as vanadium tetroxide (V_2O_4), vanadium trioxide (V_2O_3), vanadium oxide (VO), and vanadium pentoxide (V_2O_5).

Vapour pressure

It is the particle pressure of a vapour at the surface of its parent liquid.

Verdigris

It is a bright bluish-green patina which is formed on copper or bronze or brass when exposed to air or water for a long timespan, and is used as a paint pigment.

Vinegar

Obtained by fermenting dilute alcoholic liquids, this sour-tasting liquid containing acetic acid is used chiefly as a condiment and food preservative.

Vinylation

It is the introduction of a vinyl radical into a compound by reaction with acetylene.

Vitamin

It is a class of organic substances that are required in small amounts in diet for normal growth, nutrition and metabolism.

Vitreous

It refers to something which resembles glass in appearance or physical properties such as in transparency, hardness, glossiness, etc.

Voltaic cells

Also called galvanic cells, these are electrochemical cells in which spontaneous chemical reactions generate electricity.

Voltameter

Another name for coulometer, it is a scientific device, different from voltmeter, which is used for measuring and indicating the quantity of electricity.

Volumetric analysis

It is (i) the analysis of a gas by volume; (ii) the quantitative analysis by the use of exactly measured titrated volumes of standard chemical solutions or reagents.

Vulcanite

Obtained by vulcanizing natural rubber with sulphur, it is a hard, non-resilient, black vulcanized rubber, also called ebonite, is used primarily in chemical containers, electrical insulators, etc.

Vulcanisation

It is a chemical process of treating rubber or rubber like materials with sulphur or curatives at a high temperature to harden them, making them more durable materials, and improve their elasticity and strength.

❑

Washing soda

Another name for sodium carbonate, this sodium salt of carbonic acid is used for manufacturing soap powders, glass, paper, etc.

Water [H_2O]

This binary compound of hydrogen and oxygen is a colourless, transparent, odourless, tasteless liquid which exists in the form of seas, lakes, rivers, and rain. It is also present on earth in its solid and gaseous state.

Water equivalent

It is the amount of water that would absorb the same amount of heat as the calorimeter per degree temperature increase.

Water gas

Obtained by passing steam over incandescent coke, it is a flammable, toxic, synthesis gas comprising chiefly of carbon monoxide and hydrogen.

Water glass

Commonly known as sodium silicate, this substance is known in the form of solution and in solid state as well, and is used in cements, automobiles, etc.

Water of crystallisation

It refers to the water that is present in hydrated compounds or that which occurs in crystals.

Wax

Occurring naturally as a mineral or in plants and animals, this white, translucent, moldable, solid substance, which is insoluble in water, is used in the manufacture of candles, in modelling, and polishes, etc.

Weak acid

It is an acid that partially dissociates or ionizes only slightly in aqueous solution.

Weak electrolyte

It is a substance that conducts electricity poorly in a dilute aqueous solution.

Weak field ligand

It is a ligand that exerts a weak crystal or ligand field and usually forms high spin complexes with metals.

Weston cell

Named after Edward Weston, this standard voltaic cell generates a highly stable voltage suitable for calibration of voltmeters.

White spirit

Synonymous with turpentine substitute, this highly refined distillate consisting of colourless hydrocarbons is used in paint thinners, for dry-cleaning purposes, etc.

Wolframite [WO_4]

Obtained from quartz veins related to granitic rocks, it is an iron manganese tung state mineral, which is black-brown in colour, and is the chief ore of tungsten.

Wood's metal

Also known as Lipowitz's alloy, it is a fusible, eutectic alloy consisting of bismuth plus lead, tin and cadmium.

Work hardening

Also called strain hardening, it refers to the strengthening of a material by repeated plastic deformation, resulting in a distortion of its crystal structure.

Wrought iron

Made by puddling pig iron when molten, it is a tough, malleable kind of iron with a low carbon content, which is used mainly as a building material.

❑

Xanthate

It is a salt or ester of xanthic acid.

Xanthene

It is a yellowish crystalline heterocyclic compound, which is used for a range of dyes such as fluorescein and eosin.

Xanthic acid [$C_3H_6S_2O$]

It is a class of unstable organic acids consisting of sulphur, the methyl and ethyl esters of which are colourless, oily liquids with a strong smell.

Xenon [Xe]

Occurring in the earth's atmosphere in minute amounts, this colourless, odourless, heavy, inert gaseous element of the noble gases group of atomic number 54 is used in some specialized flashtubes, thyratons, etc.

X-rays

It is a form of electromagnetic radiation of short wavelength (in the range of 0.01 to 10 nanometers).

Xylenol

Derived as a crystalline substance, it is any one of six metameric phenol derivatives of xylene.

❑

Ylide

It is a neutral dipolar molecule with a formal positive and a negative charge on adjacent atoms.

Ytterbium [Yb]

Occurring naturally as minerals (gadolinite, monazite and xenotime), it is a soft, silvery-white metallic element of the lanthanide series of atomic number 70.

Yttrium [Y]

It is a silvery metallic element of atomic number 39, which is used in magnesium and aluminum alloys.

❑

Zeolite

Found in cavities in lava flows and in plutonic rocks, it is a class of microporous, glassy, aluminosilicate minerals of calcium, sodium or potassium commonly used in detergents, construction, medicines, etc.

Zinc [Zn]

Occurring in association with other base metals (copper and lead in ores), this silvery-white, lustrous, brittle metallic element of atomic number 30 is used in a wide variety of alloys and in coating iron.

Zincate

It is a salt of zinc hydroxide consisting of $ZnCOH)_4^{2-}$.

Zircon

Occurring in small prismatic crystals, this mineral, consisting of zirconium silicate, is the chief ore of zirconium, and is used as a refractory, gemstone, etc.

Zirconium [Zr]

Derived mainly from zircon, this lustrous, grey, hard metallic element of the transition series of atomic number 40 is used in nuclear reactors, alloys, etc.

Zone refining

It is a technique of purifying a bar of metal by passing it through an induction heater.

❑❑❑